Contents

Introduction

When you are called to audition, you will either be asked to do a 'cold' reading or perform something from your audition repertoire. You'll certainly need a handful of pieces under your belt, whether it's the usual 'one classical and one contemporary piece' for drama school entry or a piece for a specific audition.

Your job at an audition is not only to show that you might be right for *this particular job*, but that you are an artist with talent and imagination – so even if you are not 'right' this time round you will stick in the director's mind when she/he's casting again.

This is a selection of classical texts ranging from Aeschylus to Chekhov. Even if you don't have an audition coming up it's valuable experience to research a play and learn a speech. (One young actor I know was asked for nine audition pieces over the course of three recalls for a repertory season, so you can never have too many pieces.) Practise them regularly so you are not caught on the hop when the phone rings. It keeps your mind alive and your creative juices flowing.

So how does acting in the classics differ from acting in modern plays, and how do you choose a part that's right for you?

When you are choosing your classical repertoire, think carefully about how many pieces you need and what you are auditioning for. No good wheeling out your Jacobean revenge tragedy for an audition for *The Relapse* or helpful to render your poetic lord if you are fully forty-two and look like an escapee from *EastEnders*. Even when auditioning for the classics you still need to find something appropriate – a role for which you might actually be considered. I know, I know, you become an actor to demonstrate your versatility and transform from within. Nevertheless, you are still limited by age, experience, education, class, vocal range and physical appearance, so be realistic. After all, these are the unique raw materials of your art. Nobody else is like you.

When I was writing my book *Make Acting Work*, I had an

interesting chat with Jude Kelly (former Artistic Director of the West Yorkshire Playhouse) about 'typecasting' – unpopular as it is. I'll quote it again because you might bear it in mind when deciding which pieces to choose.

> It's very hard to make actors understand that you are often not turning them down because they are less good than somebody else – you turn them down because they are not . . . right in some way. Actors get very upset about this and yet if you ask them what they think of such and such a production, they often say, 'So and so was completely wrong for that part.' At the same time they will be arguing for a completely level playing field without any version of 'typecasting' at all . . .

Classical texts present different challenges to actors from modern ones, making greater demands on stamina, imagination, vocal flexibility and breath control. Make sure you keep fit and do your breathing exercises every day so you are in good shape – something every actor should be doing anyway. The characters use language that is alien, syntax with which we are not familiar and words that are not in our vocabulary. Sometimes texts are written in verse; language is heightened and carries complex, lengthy thought processes, imposing another range of problems. If the text is written in verse do you sacrifice its structure, rhymes and rhythms to a more colloquial tone? How do you sustain the measure and cadence of the poetry but at the same time expose the layers of emotion and meaning it carries? How can you make these texts communicate to modern audiences? How do we make these seemingly 'larger than life' characters live and breathe when their situations and modes of expression seem so unfamiliar? Just how much breath do you *need* to carry sense across five lines of iambic pentameter? No wonder actors approach classical texts with trepidation.

You won't expect me to write an essay on classical acting in an audition book, but I can give you a few tips that might help with these speeches. A couple of minutes is a short space of time for you to 'strut your stuff', so I hope my comments will help maximise your opportunities. I have tried to give you as much information as I can in the commentaries about context, and supply meanings for words and expressions not in common usage. The following is an adjunct to these.

- Read the play. You can't hope to glean all you need to know about a character and his situation from a single speech, or indeed from my commentaries.
- Learn the text accurately (you can't paraphrase Congreve or improvise iambic pentameter) and find out every last thing you can about your character and his journey through the play. Where are you? Where have you come from? Where are you headed? What do other characters have to say about you? Where does the character hail from and what accent might he use? Research the period, the social mores and the costume. What your character is wearing will make a difference to your posture and demeanour – you can't put your hands in your pockets with lacy cuffs. What do you want? Money? Power? Love? What drives you? Lust? Hatred? Ambition? Revenge? Why are you saying this now? What is your relationship with the person you are talking to? Lover? Enemy? Rival? Or, indeed, with the audience? Maybe you are alone onstage, talking to yourself, admitting the audience right inside your head, making them privy to your innermost thoughts and conflicts, or making a direct address, treating them like friends, co-conspirators or confidants? Sharing your glee? Seeking their approval? Perhaps you are stepping out of the action to make an observation to them that other characters can't hear? What is the style of the play? Where is it set? Is it a comedy or a tragedy? All this needs careful thought.
- Play the situation. Play the intention. Play the relationship. If you find the text difficult, translate it into colloquial English. Speak it aloud then return to the original with your 'translation' in mind. Rehearse until it sits easily on your tongue. Make sure you understand it. Unpick it and struggle with it until you do. You can't make an audience understand what you don't completely understand yourself. Nor can you make any emotional

connection with it. If the text is obscure, the subtext must be crystal. What do you actually mean by what you say? Characters interact and express themselves via means other than text.

- If the text is written in verse, tune your ear to its rhythms, rhymes and resonance; observe the punctuation, the length of lines and line endings – these often give clues to emphasis, changes of gear, the pace at which a character speaks, thought transitions or watchful silences. Note repetitions or where a regular rhythm changes and ask yourself why this might be. For instance, take this powerful rhyming couplet from Pheres' speech to his son in Euripides' *Alcestis*. What can we learn from unpicking it?

> 'Not die for thee?' . . . I asked not thee to die.
> Thou lovest this light: shall I not love it, I? . . .

Read it aloud – strictly observing the rhythm. It is iambic pentameter, isn't it? Read it again carefully, observing the punctuation. What does the first sentence tell us? It is short and punchy. To the point. Hard-hitting therefore. It is a question and it is in quotation marks. Pheres is quoting his son's words back at him, questioning their validity. Asking someone to die for you is a pretty outrageous request, especially your father. Look at the ellipsis after the question, giving Pheres' outrage time to register. How can you ask that of me? Did I ask it of you? Look at the weight the colon gives to the sentiment preceding it in line two. It is a matter of fact. 'You like being alive.' Then the repetition of 'I', the comma after 'it', the rhyme with the first line. Is there a sense of self-questioning here? Is Pheres wondering if he should have sacrificed himself? Why 'shall' and not 'should'? What potency the measured iambics, the rhyme and repetition give the lines. The intensity of the old man's feelings resonates through them.

> 'Not die for thee?' I asked not thee to die.
> Thou lovest this light, should I not love it too?

Not quite the same, is it?

Thus an enormous amount of information can be wrested from even a very small amount of text with minimum knowledge of its context. It is careful work that will reward your efforts.

Not too many of us experience slaughtering a Scottish king like Macbeth does but we can understand the ambition that drives him. It doesn't take a leap of imagination to put yourself in his shoes. The characters might be larger than life, their emotions heightened, the language from another age, but these plays were written to be spoken by actors just like you to convey passions no different from our own. They haven't lasted down the centuries without having something pretty powerful to say to audiences today.

My commentaries should not be seen as 'giving direction' in anything but the loosest sense. It is up to you to do your own research and bring your own interpretation to these wonderful roles. There is no 'right way' to play them, and a director will always prick up his ears if you are able to offer an original 'take' on a well-known piece. I have tried to give a few tips and indicators about background, context, interpretation and approach – to point you towards a few clues buried in the language, the structure or the syntax. I have left in stage directions where they seem relevant. Sometimes I have included the whole of a long speech so you can see the 'through line' and then cut it yourself, and on the odd occasion I have linked speeches where the thought process can be sustained when the interlocutor is cut out. I hope you will find this an interesting and varied selection. But more importantly, I hope they help to get that job. Good luck.

This book is dedicated to the memory of my friends Linda Gardner, Caroline Bingham and Carl Forgione, who enriched my life and died too soon.

Messenger from *Persians* by Aeschylus (translated by Frederic Raphael and Kenneth McLeish)

Persians is probably the oldest surviving play in Western literature (472 BC). It is a dramatic poem set at the time of the Persian Wars in the court of King Xerxes and his mother Queen Atossa. After fifty years of warfare during which the Persian Empire attempted to conquer Greece, the Persians are finally defeated. Xerxes has been tricked by a 'double agent' into launching an invasion against Athens, but in spite of the Persian army's superior numbers, their ships are trapped in a narrow strait between the island of Salamis and the mainland. Thousands of men are ambushed and slaughtered by a small advance party of Greeks. The ragged survivors, including the dishonoured Xerxes, flee in panic and attempt to return home. Many perish on the journey. The Messenger is one of the few to reach Persia. Exhausted, hungry and in a desperate state, he arrives at the palace to bring the news that almost the entire Persian army has been crushed.

This scene is near the beginning of the play. The Messenger is delivering news that has been desperately awaited – but the news is not good. He pulls no punches. His description of the Persian defeat is vivid, graphic – an eyewitness report. It feels as if we are watching an epic film. The whole course of the battle is described, frame by frame. Look how he sets the scene from the first moment Xerxes is duped by the Athenian, setting off this train of terrible events. He tells us everything. Xerxes' instructions to his captains – word for word. (How can he know this? Is he a captain himself?) The rising and setting of the sun. The men's preparations on the eve of battle. The evocation of the longboats rowing across the strait and the men's calling to each other in the dark, brave fighters nerving themselves for war – until all hell is let loose and the Greeks attack out of nowhere. Horror is heaped on horror, sorrow is heaped on sorrow in a rising crescendo of destruction and blood until the final showdown when the Persian fleet is smashed and dismembered, and corpses pile up on the shore – the Persians netted like so many fish.

The role of the Messenger in Greek tragedy is a familiar one. He is a vehicle for telling us about events that have taken place offstage. Evoke the scene for us. Engage us in the story. Make us relive the horror as if we are participants in it ourselves.

Messenger

Some demon, Majesty, some spite began disaster.
A man came to your son – a Greek, an Athenian.
Greek nerve would never hold, he said.
As soon as darkness fell, they'd leap on board,
Grab oars and row for their lives
In all directions. Xerxes believed him.
Why should he suspect the hand of God?
He sent word to all his captains. 'As soon
As the Sun withdraws his shafts that light the Earth,
As soon as darkness tenants the evening sky,
Action stations! Divide the fleet in three.
One group row round the island. The rest
Block access to open water. If any Greeks slip past,
If they trick any ships to freedom,
Your heads shall pay for it.' Proud orders:
How could he know what future gods had planned?
Our men, obedient, well-trained, ate dinner,
Then each sailor looped and tied his oar in place.
As soon as the Sun's bright light declined
And night crept in, each master-oarsman,
Each man-at-arms, embarked. The longships sailed.
Calling out to one another, they rowed
In line ahead across the strait. As ordered,
The captains kept them rowing to and fro
All night. All night –
And not one glimpse of Greeks!
Day dawned. White horses streaked the sky.
Light dazzled – and a huge Greek shout,
Crashing, echoing. We cowered:
Our plan had made us clowns.
These were no runaways, shrieking for safety;
These were fighters, nerving themselves for war.
The trumpet flamed and fired their ranks.
Their oars flayed sea to foam. Fast, fast they came,
Parading for battle: the right wing first,

The rest in good order. And all the time
From every throat, we heard their battle-cry:
'On, sons of Greece! Set free
Your fatherland, your children, wives,
Homes of your ancestors and temples of your gods!
Save all, or all is lost!'
On our side a roar, a tide of answering cries.
The fight began. Ship pounced on ship.
Bronze beaks stripped wood. First blood to Greece:
An Athenian warship rammed its prey,
A galleon from Tyre, sheared all its poop away.
Now, full ahead, ship skewered ship. At first
Our Persian fleet held firm. But soon
Ships choked the straits; no room to turn, to help.
Oars smashed; sterns caved in;
The bronze beaks bit and bit.
The Greeks snatched their advantage,
Surrounding us, pounding us.
Ship after ship capsized;
The sea was swamped with wreckage, corpses,
The beaches, dunes, all piggy-backed with dead.
Our ships broke ranks, tried one by one
To slip the line. The Greeks, like fishermen
With a haul of tunny netted and trapped,
Stabbed, gaffed with snapped-off oars
And broken spars, smashed, smashed, till all the sea
Was one vast salty soup of shrieks and cries.
At last black night came down and hid the scene.
Disaster on disaster. I could take ten days,
And not tell all. Be sure of this: never before
Have so many thousands died on a single day.

Pheres from *Alcestis* by Euripides
(translated by Gilbert Murray)

First performed in 438 BC, *Alcestis* takes place in and around the castle of Admetus, King of Pherae, in Thessaly.

The play opens with the god Apollo telling the audience how he has negotiated with the underworld to spare Admetus' life if someone else will die in his place. The only volunteer is his loyal wife, Alcestis. His father and mother, whom Admetus might have expected to volunteer, have refused the service. Thanatos, Death's messenger, has collected his victim and the household is in mourning for Alcestis, who is being buried with honours and ceremony.

Pheres, Admetus' infirm old father, the former King of Pherae, has brought robes and gifts to be buried with his beloved daughter-in-law. He praises her sacrifice for not leaving him childless in his dotage, but Admetus overhears him and renounces him for not doing the decent thing and offering himself. After all, he doesn't have much time left anyway. Pheres rounds on him with righteous indignation, delivering a few painful home truths – calling him a 'coward' and a 'pretty soldier' – and demolishing Admetus' arguments with biting and measured fury – outraged by his son's dishonourable and uncaring behaviour. It is Admetus who is responsible for Alcestis' death, not he. What right has Admetus to ask him to die if he is not prepared to die himself? Hasn't he given him everything else?

The play has been translated into simple rhyming verse, which gives Pheres indignation, great power and intensity. Look at the punctuation and repetitions. Note how carefully Pheres chooses and weighs his words: 'Thou lovest the light: shall I not love it, I? . . .', 'My sunlit time is short, but dear; but dear.'

Admetus will return from the burial a changed man, shamed by Pheres into the painful acknowledgement that he has not only lost his beloved wife but his honour too.

Pheres

My son, whom seekest thou . . . some Lydian thrall,
Or Phrygian, bought with cash? . . . to affright withal
By cursing? I am a Thessalian, free,
My father a born chief of Thessaly;
And thou most insolent. Yet think not so
To fling thy loud lewd words at me and go.
   I got thee to succeed me in my hall,
I have fed thee, clad thee. But I have no call
To die for thee. Not in our family,
Not in all Greece, doth law bid fathers die
To save their sons. Thy road of life is thine,
None other's, to rejoice at or repine.
All that was owed to thee by us is paid.
My throne is thine. My broad lands shall be made
Thine, as I had them from my father . . . Say,
How have I wronged thee? What have I kept away?
'Not died for thee?' . . . I ask not thee to die.
   Thou lovest this light: shall I not love it, I? . . .
'Tis age on age there, in the dark; and here
My sunlit time is short, but dear; but dear.
   Thou hast fought hard enough. Thou drawest breath
Even now, long past thy portioned hour of death,
By murdering her . . . and blamest my faint heart,
Coward, who hast let a woman play thy part
And die to save her pretty soldier! Aye,
A good plan, surely! Thou needst never die;
Thou canst find always somewhere some fond wife
To die for thee. But, prithee, make not strife
With other friends, who will not save thee so.
Be silent, loving thine own life, and know
All men love theirs! . . . Taunt others, and thou too
Shalt hear much that is bitter, and is true.

Messenger from *Medea* by Euripides (translated by J. Michael Walton)

This tragedy of 431 BC focuses on a woman whose jealousy and desire for revenge are unbounded when she discovers her husband Jason has traded her in for a younger model.

Jason is deprived of his kingdom of Thessaly by his brother, Pelias. In order to regain it, he is required to fetch the fabled Golden Fleece from the King of Colchis. He sets sail, and after many hair-raising adventures captures the fleece with the aid of Medea, who uses sorcery to help him, then betrays her father and murders her brother. The couple marry and return to Greece with their two sons where Medea again uses her powers to have Pelias killed, but still the throne eludes them and they are forced to flee to Corinth. Once there, the ambitious Jason deserts her for Glauke, the Princess of Corinth, in order to 'naturalise' and consolidate his position. Fearful that Medea will seek revenge, Glauke's father, Creon, tries to banish her and the children before the wedding, but Medea tricks him into allowing her to stay one more day so that she can make proper provision for their departure. Creon's agreement has the direst consequences.

Medea wishes the couple well and sends a wedding present to Glauke via the children. It is a bewitched crown and gown that will seer into Glauke's skull and flay her flesh when she puts it on, causing a slow, terrible death.

She dispatches her messenger to go to the palace and report back on what the bride was wearing. He returns in disarray to tell her that Creon and Glauke have died from her sorcery. It is music to Medea's ears and she commands him to relate the whole story of their deaths and suffering.

The Greeks made no attempt to portray violence onstage so the Messenger is a device to provide vivid word pictures of offstage events. He should be made flesh and blood as he describes the happy atmosphere of the festivities, then the horror when she dons the poisoned dress and crown. The story should move and chill the heart. The actor must convey the Messenger's disgust at Medea's heartlessness; he should shock and transfix us with the horror of what he has just seen, as if it had just happened in front of us.

Messenger

When the children, those two boys of yours,
Arrived with their father at the palace,
They found it all decorated for the wedding,
And us servants, who used to take your side,
We were delighted. Word had got around, you see,
That you and your husband had been reconciled.
People shook the boys' hands or patted their golden hair.
I was so excited I followed them to the women's rooms.
The princess – she has our allegiance now, not you –
She turned her gaze on Jason lovingly
Until she caught sight of the two children,
Then turned away and wouldn't look at them,
White as a sheet, furious to find them there.
Your husband tried to placate her, saying,
'Don't be angry. Look. They only want to love you.
Your husband's friends must be your friends too.
They've brought presents. Accept them.
And ask your father to reprieve them. For me?'
The moment she saw the finery, she couldn't resist,
And gave in to all he asked.
Father and son were barely out the door
Before she snatched the gorgeous dress and put it on,
Then the gold coronet, checking in the mirror,
Giggling at the reflection of herself
As she arranged her curls round the tiara.
Then up she jumped from her dressing-table
And prinked around the room on her little white feet,
Glorying in her presents, again and again,
Posing, checking from head to heel.
Then, all of a sudden, something dreadful.
She changed colour, staggered,
Started to shiver, managed just
To fall on the bed, not on the floor.
An old servant mumbled a prayer,
Assuming some god-frenzy or a fit.

But one look at her mouth –
Froth was bubbling from her lips,
Eyes rolling, colour drained.
No prayer then but a howl.
Someone ran for her father,
Someone else for the new husband,
To tell them what was happening to the bride,
The corridors echoing with running feet.
For the time it takes a runner to complete a lap
She lay mute, poor woman,
Then started up, eyes tight shut, with a scream,
Ravaged by a double torture.
From the golden crown about her hair,
Flames shot, burning, ghastly.
But on her body so soft, the soft dress
That the children had brought began to feed.
She rose, ran, on fire,
Tossing her head every way,
To shake off that halo. But it clung.
The more she shook, the more it flared.
Seared to the bone, at last she fell to the ground.
A father might recognise her, only a father.
You couldn't pick out her eyes,
Her features. Just blood dripping
From her head on to the flickering flames.
While her flesh, gorged on by the poison,
Dribbled off her like gum from a pine.
Horrible. I can see it. No one dared touch her.
We were witnesses. We'd learned.
But her poor father knew nothing of this.
Rushing in he threw himself on her body,
Weeping, clinging to her, crying
'Child, poor child, who or what has destroyed you?
Who's turned this old man into a gravestone?
Oh child, let me die too.'
Eventually his sobbing began to subside

And he started to try to get up.
But as he'd clung to her, she clung to him,
Like ivy clings to the laurel.
So with her dress he began a ghastly wrestling-match.
As he scrabbled to get to his knees,
She seemed to reach and grab him.
He fought her off and the flesh stripped from his bones.
At last – it took time – the wretched man
Succumbed to his fate and gave up the ghost.
The corpses lie together, child and father, close.
'Let me die too.' The release of tears he craved.

And your part in this? I've said nothing.
You'll have secured your own escape.
'Walking shadows', that's all we are.
And so-called clever men, the silver-tongued –
I'm not afraid to admit it – pay too. They pay.
Call no man happy. That's what I say.
You might be luckier than your neighbour,
Be more prosperous. But happy? Never.

Manservant from *Medea* by Euripides (adapted by Liz Lochhead)

This is Liz Lochhead's Scots take on the same speech. While her version pays homage to its source, and adheres to the original structure, it is an interpretation rather than a translation and packs a powerful contemporary punch with its portrayal of Scots culture and prejudice. In Lochhead's own words, 'The Athenian (male) society of his time which Euripides scourged for its smug and conventional attitudes of unthinking superiority to foreigners and women is unfortunately not totally unrecognisable . . . two and a half thousand years later.'

For the background story, read the commentary for the previous extract.

This version uses Scots vernacular for the dominant society, while Medea speaks with the 'foreign-speaking-good-English' of a refugee and 'incomer'. Unlike the original, she has a daughter as well as sons. This Manservant is handsome, young, strong and macho – something of a trusted confidant, faithful, discreet and not immune to Medea's charms. He has a strong accent, using many words from the Scots dialect. He's 'no much of a man for describing frocks' but Medea has no trouble in persuading him to go back to the palace to check out the bride's outfit. When he sees the impact of Medea's deadly sorcery he runs back to her in a terrible state, gasping in terror. She demands that he tell her everything he has seen, impatient to relish her success. Look how the speech is laid out – with hardly any punctuation and gaps where he tries to catch his breath. He knows Jason will mete out a terrible revenge and is terrified both for his mistress's safety and his own. Medea's old nurse is frozen to the spot, also terrified. He tries to shake her into action, before fleeing in a directionless panic.

I have given the whole speech, but you may want to cut it for an audition.

Manservant

the ceremony was done
Kreon kissed his daughter
shook the hand of her new husband
and took his leave
mindan the company how   in the great hall
there wad be feasting later
in the meantime there was dancing
whistling and cheering   applause from us servants
when the happy couple took the floor thegether

then did the bride's eye no alight
on the crown your lassie'd brocht her?
nothing for it but she left her husband's side
laughing   ran and took it up
set it   gold on gold   on tap of her hair
when she pulled oot that soft silk shawl
there was a sigh went up at its shimmer
and she slipped into it
smoothing it over her breasts and shooders
Jason whistled   she shimmied to the mirror
and stopped   stilled by her own
silvered beauty in the glass
stared smiling   totally taen on wi hersel
as why should she no be?

then – something hellish – before our eyes
her face cheynged colour   she swayed   reeled
across the floor   her legs buckling under her
only just made it to a chair
one of her servin lassies thought she was
only carrying on   that it was a joke
she whooped   then she saw
that her majesty was foaming at the mouth and
her eyes turned all milky and opaque flickering
wi the pupils rolled back   and the colour she was
which was the colour of clay   of death
but she was gasping

ripping scarves of breath from the air
drawing them into her lungs
drowning   the servin lass cheynged her tune then
the shriek she let out   Gods   it made
all our blood run cold
stuck there as we were like stookies
wi the horror of it   then it was all running feet
everywhere and the palace rang with shouts as they
tore the place apart looking for her faither

Jason just stood there   that look on his face
one I hope never to see on another human face again

for the length of time it takes a good runner
to lap the racetrack she was slumped unconscious
then she found her voice   her eyes bulged
she began to scream and scream
for a twofold agony began to attack her
on her head that golden circlet
became a filigree of flame melting and dripping
liquid fire   and the silky shawl
the other present from the children
began to shrivel   suck   and paste itself
to her skin   smothering her   strangling
branding her soft flesh
as if she was fire itsel   she leapt
rolling in agony   trying to put herself out
no one but her father would have known her
blebbed and burning as she was
her melting flesh falling off her bones like
tallow from a flamboy or   fat from a lamb on a spit
bubbling and bursting like
resin drops on a burning pine
till at last her horrid corpse
was blackened   silent   and still

we shrank back   we were terrified
there was none of us would touch it
we'd seen   we knew

till Kreon came   poor man
ran in   cried out   fell on the corpse
cradling it   sobbing
'Gods let me die with you!' he cried
'the parent should not outlive the child'
and he wept till his auld eyes could weep nae mair
and he was all gret oot
but when he went to staun up
here did the corpse no stick to him
as ivy clings to laurel   and it was
a dance macabre right enough
as the auld fellow tried to struggle free
and the deid weight of the deid daughter
pu'ed him to his knees again   the sair fecht of it
tearing his auld flesh from his aged bones
till at last he snuffed it   croaked
and there they lie
father on top of daughter   corpse on corpse
in a horrid parody of an unnatural embrace

the Gods are good
somebody was listening when he cried 'I want to die'
it could be said he   right royal   got his wish

and that's that
no surprise to you   Medea
by the Gods I'm feart frae you
mair feart even than I am feart o Jason
and the soldiers he'll bring with him
to torch this place

The **Manservant** *runs to the frozen-in-fear* **Nurse** *and shakes her.*

they'll kill us
I don't think we have snowball in hell's chance
but we maun
run auld yin   run

Agamemnon from *Iph. . .* after *Iphigenia in Aulis* by Euripides (adapted by Colin Teevan)

First performed in Athens in 405 BC, a couple of years after Euripides' death, *Iphigenia in Aulis* has since become one of the most performed of Greek tragedies. It explores the breakdown of social norms in times of war and how 'war breeds inhuman habits in the most humane of men' – a topic still relevant today. It dramatises the myth of Iphigeneia who was sacrificed to the gods by her father, Agamemnon, in order to facilitate victory over Troy.

Commander of the Greek armies, Agamemnon is both a brilliant military strategist and a ruthless murderer and wife abuser. Agamemnon's fleet has been stranded for weeks in the bay of Aulis by bad weather. In revenge for killing one of her sacred stags, the angry goddess Artemis has demanded the sacrifice of the virginal Iphigeneia, to appease her and provide a fair wind for the expedition.

Agamemnon summons Iphigeneia on the pretence that she is to marry her hero the warrior Achilleus, who knows nothing of this, but he has second thoughts. His brother, Menelaus (whose wife has been taken to Troy by Paris, precipitating the war), threatens to tell the restless troops of his cowardice if he does not proceed as planned. He is cornered into going ahead with the sacrifice.

Here, Iphigeneia has just arrived to a big welcoming committee. Much to Agamemnon's consternation, her mother, Klytaimnestra, has also come, to help with the 'wedding'. What can he tell them? He presents himself as a man in thrall to fate and the cunning of the gods who are toying with his life; a great man who cannot be seen to be vacillating or weak; a man caught on the horns of a huge moral dilemma. His anguish is on full display. Nevertheless, we know he is capable of great cruelty to further his own interests – prepared to commit this atrocious act to save face, further his military ambitions and secure victory.

Agamemnon

And what am I supposed to tell them?
It's too late for turning back. Too late.
You Gods,
How cleartell this heartache?
How begin to break the binds
Of these threads in which I'm now entwined?
Some God plays with me and my plans,
His cunning far outwits my petty wiles.
The rabble live with lighter load,
Unencumbered, they can cry
When the fates fuck them around.
Not so us people of position,
We must appearances preserve.
We are the slaves of our supporters.
Trapped helpless in their gaze.
What can I do?
I am ashamed to show my grief,
Yet it is shameful not to shed a tear,
Such misfortunes now enmesh me.
You Gods, were things not bad enough
Without Klytaimnestra coming too?
With what words will I greet my wife?
With what face can I look at her?
A mother must tend to her daughter, I suppose,
On her daughter's wedding day.
Though this father grieves at how
He must give his child away.
My child,
My ill-starred child,
Who will now honeymoon with Hades.
On her knees she'll beg me;
Father, do not marry me to martyrdom, Papa –

Philolaches from *The Haunted House* by Plautus (translated by Kenneth McLeish and Michael Sargent)

The plays of the comic dramatist Titus Maccius Plautus were first produced between 205 and 184 BC and are the earliest surviving works from Roman literature.

This is something of a farce in which the main character is the clever slave, Tranio, who corrupts his young Athenian master, Philolaches, during his father's lengthy absence on a business trip. Plautus uses an Athenian setting to highlight and reinforce the good Roman values, by contrasting them with the decadence of the Greeks.

Tranio has promised Philolaches' father, Theopropides, that he will look after the house while he is away, but instead he has eaten him out of house and home and enjoyed the high life at his expense. His transgressions include drunkenness, whoring, extravagance and encouraging Philolaches to join him in his debauched lifestyle.

Philolaches is a handsome, once-promising young man from a rich family, but under his machinating slave's tutelage has 'gone to the bad'. He has fallen far short of the 'Roman values' expected of him. He is gullible, easily led, rather 'public school', a bit wet and not overly bright. In this inebriated address to the audience, he assesses his moral decline, comparing it to a house that has fallen into disrepair through long-term neglect. It is a diatribe of fatuous bar-room philosophy presented as intelligent argument. Look how he repeats himself or says the same thing in several different ways, overemphasising points he wants to make – drunkenly leaning into the audience to share his 'meaningful' discovery. He has been enjoying himself with Tranio, wasted vast sums of money and run up huge debts to buy the freedom of a scheming young slave girl he is besotted with. This passion has only compounded his decline. He knows he is beyond redemption, but has he really learned anything? Probably not.

This is not a speech with a complicated subtext but you can certainly mine the comic potential of Philolaches' dissipated ramblings.

When Theopropides returns unexpectedly in the middle of a drunken party, Tranio invents a ludicrous story about hauntings and ghosts to keep him out of the house. But the pair's schemes are finally revealed when a moneylender turns up and blows the gaff, and subsequent machinations to cover their tracks become unstuck. All ends happily, though, when Theopropides is persuaded to forgive them both for their outrages and Tranio lives to sin another day.

Philolaches   You know, there's a matter I've been giving a lot of thought to lately . . . arguing it through with myself . . . a lot of heart-searching . . . that's if I have anything that can be called a heart. It's this: after much pondering and cogitation, I've come to the conclusion that MAN IS . . . well, any man, that is, whatever his station in life . . . MAN IS RATHER LIKE . . . or, at least, IS NOT UNLIKE . . . or, let's say, he SOMEWHAT RESEMBLES . . . at least I think I'll be able to convince you of this . . . when you've heard my arguments . . . MAN IS (when he's first born, that is) LIKE A NEW HOUSE. Mmmm!

Now I dare say that you don't immediately notice the similarity, but I hope . . . in fact, I'm sure that you'll agree with me . . . when you've heard what I have to say, that is. So listen carefully while I explain . . . I don't want to keep this all to myself, I want you all to share my great discovery.

So, A HOUSE. When a nice new house is built, properly finished, constructed to a T, as they say . . . well, it may not actually be a T, it might be some other shape, but you know what I mean . . . everyone likes it, they say the builders have done a splendid job, everyone wants it, or rather wants one just like it, and they start saving up so they can buy something similar. But let's say the owner is some idle, careless, good-for-nothing, lazy slob. What happens? The house begins to suffer. There's a storm . . . wind and rain . . . tiles fall off, roofs leak (and the owner does nothing about it), rain comes washing down the walls, drips through the ceilings, the rafters start to rot, all the builder's work is ruined. Things go from bad to worse . . . it's not the builder's fault, of course, a little bit of care and money could have stopped the damage, but they put it off and put it off and do nothing and . . . CRASH!!! . . . the whole house collapses . . . and there's nothing for it but to rebuild the whole thing from scratch.

Right! So that's a house. Now I want to go on and explain why I think a MAN is like a HOUSE. Well, in the first place, parents are the builders . . . of their children. They lay the foundations, raise the structure up, guide its growth, spare no expense. They want it to be a credit to them. They teach them respect, what's right and wrong.

They want their neighbours to envy them and wish they had children like that.

But sooner or later the boy leaves home . . . military service, perhaps . . . the builder loses sight of him. What happens to the building then?

Take me, for example. I was always a steady, serious-minded chap, when I was in the builders' hands. But left to my own devices . . . well, it didn't take me long to undo all their work and make the house a ruin. Rainy weather . . . that was idleness. Gales and hailstorms . . . carelessness and indifference. I did nothing to repair the damage. And then came LOVE . . . pouring into my heart and soul. I was flooded out. Goodbye to fortune, faith, my reputation, my honour! My house is beyond repair, nothing can stop it becoming a total ruin.

It makes me very sad to see what I am now, and what I was. I was a model child, top of the class in games and exercises, an example to all my friends; even the best of them said I could teach them something. Now . . . I'm good for nothing. That's the one thing I have taught myself.

Matthew Merrygreek from *Ralph Roister Doister* by Nicholas Udall

This is the earliest known English comedy, first performed probably in 1552 shortly before Shakespeare's birth. It is the only surviving work of Nicholas Udall, a schoolmaster, who wrote it for his pupils. It is the story of bragging hero Ralph Roister Doister and his hanger-on, Matthew Merrygreek.

Roister Doister is determined to marry widow Dame Christian Custance – more for her money than her person – and sends various messengers to woo her on his behalf. But the pious Dame is already engaged to the noble Gawyn Goodluck and will not be deflected. The comedy is rooted in Roister Doister's attempts to seek her favour and Merrygreek's mischievous efforts to thwart him.

Here, Merrygreek is setting the scene and tone of the drama – justifying his parasitical lifestyle in a direct address to the audience, shamelessly boasting about how he influences and humours his biggest patron. While he bears Roister Doister no real ill will, he has little respect for him and relishes playing on his weaknesses which he gleefully catalogues. Merrygreek is a colourful con man, a mischief-maker with an eye to every main chance. He has befriended Roister Doister as much for the fun of it as for what he can squeeze out of him. The gullible hero is putty in his hands.

Udall's characters are broadly drawn, representing their moral positions in the play, and you can deduce Merrygreek's character and lifestyle from his name (beware of Greeks bearing gifts) and the names of the company he keeps – Lewis Loiterer, Watkin Waster, Davy Diceplayer, etc. He is one half stock character from a Roman comedy (with which the classicist Udall would have been familiar), the other half, a slapstick devil representing 'Vice', a stock character from the morality plays of the Middle Ages.

This is quite challenging stuff. The dialogue is written in uneven rhyming couplets – difficult to lift from the page without slipping into a sing-song delivery. Don't let the rhyme lead you. Play Merrygreek's manipulative relish, engage the audience in his conspiratorial gossip and have fun with it.

Merrygreek

As long liveth the merry man, they say,
As doth the sorry man, and longer by a day;
Yet the grasshopper, for all his summer piping,
Starveth in winter with hungry griping.
Therefore another said saw doth men advise
That they be together both merry and wise.
This lesson must I practise, or else ere long,
With me, Matthew Merrygreek, it will be wrong.
Indeed, men so call me; for, by Him that us brought,
Whatever chance betide, I can take no thought;
Yet wisdom would that I did myself bethink
Where to be provided this day of meat and drink;
For know ye, that, for all this merry note of mine,
He might appose me now that should ask where I dine.
My living lieth here, and there, of God's grace
Sometime with this good man, sometime in that place,
Sometime Lewis Loiterer biddeth me come near;
Somewhiles Watkin Waster maketh us good cheer;
Sometimes Davy Diceplayer, when he hath well cast,
Keepeth revel-rout as long at it will last;
Sometimes Tom Titivile maketh us a feast;
Sometime with Sir Hugh Pye I am a bidden guest,
Sometime at Nicol Neverthrive's I get a sop,
Sometime I am feasted with Bryan Blinkinsop,
Sometime I hang on Hankyn Hoddydody's sleeve,
But this day, on Ralph Roister Doister's, by his leave.
For truly of all men he is my chief banker
Both for meat and money, and my chief sheet-anchor.
For, sooth Roister Doister in that he doth say,
And require what ye will, ye shall have no nay.
But now of Roister Doister somewhat to express,
That ye may esteem him after his worthiness:
In these twenty towns, and seek them throughout,
Is not the like stock whereon to graff a lout.
All the day long is he facing and craking

Of his great acts in fighting and fraymaking:
But, when Roister Doister is put to his proof,
To keep the Queen's peace is more for his behoof.
If any woman smile, or cast on him an eye,
Up is he to the hard ears in love by-and-by!
And in all the hot haste must she be his wife,
Else farewell his good days and farewell his life!
Master Ralph Roister Doister is but dead and gone
Except she on him take some compassion,
Then chief of counsel must be Matthew Merrygreek:
'What if I for marriage to seek an one seek?'
Then must I sooth it, whatever it is:
For what he saith or doth cannot be amiss.
Hold up his yea and nay, be his nown white son.
Praise and rouse him well, and ye have his heart won,
For so well liketh he his own fond fashions
That he taketh pride of false commendations.
But such sport have I with him as I would not lese,
Though I should be bound to live with bread and cheese.
For exalt him, and have him as ye lust, indeed –
Yea, to hold his finger in a hole for a need.
I can, with a word, make him fain or loth;
I can, with as much, make him pleased or wroth;
I can, when I will, make him merry and glad,
I can, when me lust, make him sorry and sad;
I can set him in hope, and eke in despair;
I can make him speak rough, and make him speak fair.
But I marvel I see him not all this same day;
I will seek him out – But, lo! he cometh this way.
I have yond espied him sadly coming,
And in love, for twenty pound, by his glumming.

---

said saw: saying
appose: embarrass
facing: swaggering
craking: boasting
behoof: liking
hard: very

then must I soth it: I must humour him
nown: own
white son: favourite
lese: lose
exalt: praise
lust: please
eke: also
glumming: frowning

Tamburlaine from *Tamburlaine the Great* by Christopher Marlowe

This play – written in two five-act parts – was first performed in London in 1587 and was possibly the opening production at the new Rose Theatre. Its heroic theme centres on the fourteenth-century Mogul conqueror, Tamburlaine, whose relentless rise to power and enormous vanity and greed resulted in his downfall.

Tamburlaine is a man of lowly birth – the son of a shepherd – an 'outsider' who sets out to conquer the Eastern world and win the love of Zenocrate, daughter of the Sultan of Egypt, whom he captures on a military raid. This is Marlowe's description in the first edition: 'Tamburlaine the Great . . . by his rare and wonderful conquests, became a most puissant and mighty monarch, and, for his tyranny and terror in war, was termed the Scourge of God.'

Marlowe's Tamburlaine – part historical, part imaginary – is capable of sickening cruelty, ruthless in the pursuit of power, treacherous and brutal to his enemies. But he is also a brilliant tactician – persuasive, eloquent, hungry for beauty and capable of great emotional depth. At the end of Part 1, after savagely conquering half the Eastern world, he marries Zenocrate in a triumphant wedding ceremony. The one thing that rivals Tamburlaine's ambition is his love for Zenocrate.

Part 2 shows us an older, more vulnerable Tamburlaine. Zenocrate is dying. She lies on her bed of state, tended by her doctors as a grieving Tamburlaine sits by her with their three sons. Written in balanced blank verse, by turn both grand and tender, this is Tamburlaine's lament for his dying wife. His grief is couched in the most resonant terms, rich with metaphysical imagery and driven by a haunting refrain (note the double meaning of 'divine') which gives the speech both symmetry and direction as he tells how the gods are preparing a celestial entertainment for Zenocrate's arrival in heaven.

This is not a soliloquy, but rather a eulogy that enlists the audience's empathy with the character's woe. It is only when we reach the last line, as he turns to her doctors to ask a rhetorical question about her health, that we seem to re-engage with the action of the play.

_____

Tamburlaine
 Black is the beauty of the brightest day;
 The golden ball of heaven's eternal fire,
 That danc'd with glory on the silver waves,
 Now wants the fuel that inflam'd his beams,
 And, all with faintness and for foul disgrace,
 He binds his temples with a frowning cloud,
 Ready to darken earth with endless night.
 Zenocrate, that gave him light and life,
 Whose eyes shot fire from their ivory bowers
 And tempered every soul with lively heat,
 Now by the malice of the angry skies,
 Whose jealousy admits no second mate,
 Draws in the comfort of her latest breath,
 All dazzled with the hellish mists of death.
 Now walk the angels on the walls of heaven
 As sentinels to warn th'immortal souls
 To entertain divine Zenocrate.
 Apollo, Cynthia, and the ceaseless lamps
 That gently look'd upon this loathsome earth
 Shine downwards now no more, but deck the heavens
 To entertain divine Zenocrate.
 The crystal springs, whose taste illuminates
 Refined eyes with an eternal sight,
 Like tried silver runs through Paradise
 To entertain divine Zenocrate.
 The cherubins and holy seraphins,
 That sing and play before the King of Kings,
 Use all their voices and their instruments
 To entertain divine Zenocrate.
 And, in this sweet and curious harmony,
 The god that tunes this music to our souls
 Holds out his hand in highest majesty
 To entertain divine Zenocrate.
 Then let some holy trance convey my thoughts
 Up to the palace of th'empyreal heaven,

That this my life may be as short to me
As are the days of sweet Zenocrate.
Physicians, will no physic do her good?

Apollo and Cynthia: the sun and moon
Tried silver: purified silver
Curious: exquisite
Th'empyreal heaven: the outermost sphere of the universe and the home of God

Black Will from *Arden of Feversham* (anon)

This domestic tragicomedy, published in 1592, is based on a notorious real-life murder committed in 1551 – 'the lamentable and true tragedy of master Arden of Feversham in Kent who was most wickedly murdered by the means of his disloyal and wanton wife who, for the love she bore to one Mosbie, hired two desperate ruffians Black Will and Shakebag to kill him'. It is an action-packed tale of strong passions, class envy, murder and greed. The question as to whether Shakespeare had a hand in it has been debated for over three centuries. There is certainly some stylistic evidence in it.

The hired killer is not known as 'Black' Will for nothing. He is a 'black-hearted' ex-army corporal, an out-and-out villain, who is quick to anger and 'would murder any man for a crown'. Here, he is talking to Greene (Alice Arden's intermediary) and Shakebag, his accomplice – after various plots and attempts to kill Arden have failed. Despite the poisoning, knifing, bludgeoning, shooting and strangling, the elusive Arden has still escaped with his life. (Will and Shakebag must be the most bumbling hit men in history, so their antics are not without a comic dimension.)

This is the talk of criminal low life in a tavern or on a street corner, and we are given a vivid picture of the underbelly of Elizabethan London. Greene is at the point of giving up on the whole business, but 'hard man' Black Will is not to be put off and boasts of a catalogue of murders, villainous deeds and protection rackets he has been involved in to demonstrate he is equal to the task. He is a man to be feared, a man for whom such matters are 'all in a day's work'. He certainly isn't going to be put off his stroke by Arden's miraculous escapes, or lose the twenty gold coins promised by Alice and Mosbie when the deed is done. It has become something of the ultimate challenge to kill his victim.

Will Thou knowest, Greene, that I have lived in London this twelve years, where I have made some go upon wooden legs for taking the wall on me; divers with silver noses for saying 'There goes Black Will!' I have cracked as many blades as thou hast done nuts. The bawdy-houses have paid me tribute; there durst not a whore set up, unless she have agreed with me first for opening her shop-windows. For a cross word of a tapster I have pierced one barrel after another with my dagger, and held him by the ears till all his beer hath run out. In Thames Street a brewer's cart was like to have run over me: I made no more ado, but went to the clerk and cut all the notches off his tallies and beat them about his head. I and my company have taken the constable from his watch, and carried him about the fields on a coltstaff. I have broken a sergeant's head with his own mace, and bailed whom I list with my sword and buckler. All the tenpenny-alehouses would stand every morning with a quart-pot in his hand, saying, 'Will it please your worship drink?' He that had not done so, had been sure to have had his sign pulled down and his lattice borne away the next night. To conclude, what have I not done? yet cannot do this; doubtless, he is preserved by miracle.

Oberon from *A Midsummer Night's Dream* by William Shakespeare

A comedy written around 1595, the action takes place on midsummer's eve, a customary time for strange and magical events. It moves between Athens and a nearby wood during the preparations for the marriage of Duke Theseus and Hippolyta. Several plots interweave involving four young lovers, preparations for the wedding entertainment by local workmen, and a quarrel between Oberon, king of the fairies, and his queen, Titania.

Their feud is over a little changeling boy in Titania's entourage whom Oberon wants as his page, but Titania has refused to hand him over. To punish her, Oberon sends Puck, a malevolent fairy, to squeeze the juice of a magic flower into Titania's eyes while she is asleep – when she wakes she will fall in love with the first thing she sees. Bottom and his fellow workmen are rehearsing their wedding entertainment in the wood. Puck thinks he's an apt subject for Oberon's practical joke, so plants an ass's head on him and charms him into falling asleep next to Titania, with predictable results.

Oberon is an imperious, supernatural fairy ruler with the power to exact anything he wants. He occupies the mysterious twilight world of the woods. (Shakespeare's fairies are not bound by human morality, laws or feelings. They can change shape, become invisible, move at the speed of light and alter the course of love and the workings of nature.)

In this scene Titania is asleep, entwined in Bottom's arms. Oberon tells Puck how he found Titania in the wood lavishing her foolish attention on him and how, under the enchantment, she has given him the changeling without a fuss. Having got what he wants he has begun to feel a bit sorry for the trick he has played, although he shares a certain malicious glee with Puck over their success. Now he has his way he is prepared to undo the spell – remorse is clearly not a fairy trait! He tells Puck to remove the ass's head, then chants a spell over his sleeping queen to release her from the bewitching love-juice and wake her up.

Oberon (*advancing*)

Welcome, good Robin.

Seest thou this sweet sight?

Her dotage now I do begin to pity;

For, meeting her of late behind the wood,

Seeking sweet favours for this hateful fool,

I did upbraid her and fall out with her.

For she his hairy temples then had rounded

With coronet of fresh and fragrant flowers;

And that same dew which sometime on the buds

Was wont to swell like round and orient pearls

Stood now within the pretty flowerets' eyes,

Like tears that did their own disgrace bewail.

When I had at my pleasure taunted her,

And she in mild terms begg'd my patience,

I then did ask of her changeling child;

Which straight she gave me, and her fairy sent

To bear him to my bower in fairy land.

And now I have the boy, I will undo

This hateful imperfection of her eyes.

And, gentle Puck, take this transformed scalp

From off the head of this Athenian swain,

That he awaking when the other do

May all to Athens back again repair,

And think no more of this night's accidents

But as the fierce vexation of a dream.

But first I will release the Fairy Queen.

(*Touching her eyes.*)

Be as thou wast wont to be;

See as thou was wont to see.

Dian's bud o'er Cupid's flower

Hath such force and blessed power.

Now, my Titania; wake you, my sweet queen.

Robin (Goodfellow): another name for Puck

Dian's bud: a herb associated with the goddess Diana which was supposed to preserve chastity

Cupid's flower: the 'little western flower' Puck used to put the spell on Titania

Simon Eyre from *The Shoemaker's Holiday* by Thomas Dekker

This joyous domestic comedy, written around 1599, is about a group of shoemakers living and working in the city of London, and the rising star of master shoemaker, Simon Eyre, who through good fortune and good investment becomes Lord Mayor. It captures all the atmosphere of Elizabethan London life and the business of a shoemaker's workshop. It also concerns the love affair between Rowland Lacy, nephew of the Earl of Lincoln, and Rose, pretty daughter of Sir Roger Oateley. Uncle and father both object to the union and, to separate them, Oateley sends his daughter to the country and Lincoln secures an army command for his nephew in the French wars. But love will not be thwarted and Lacy arranges for a cousin to take over his command and, disguising himself as Hans, a Dutch shoemaker (a trade he has learned on the Continent), goes to London. He finds employment in Simon Eyre's shop and after many lively and fast-moving plot twists the couple are reunited. Just as they are about to marry Lincoln tracks them down, but Eyre, now Lord Mayor of London, promises the couple protection under the wings of his new office.

Simon Eyre is an energetic and broadly drawn man in his fifties – a good-hearted tradesman, 'a man of the best presence', 'a true shoemaker and gentleman of the Gentle Craft'. He is benign, eloquent, affable and egalitarian – a fair-minded employer and a devoted husband to Margery (now elevated to Mayoress Lady Madgy). He wears his new office with great dignity and geniality, the perfect model of the rising middle class.

This scene takes place on the morning of the couple's marriage. They are worried that something will go wrong at the last minute, but Eyre puts aside their doubts and reassures them that, as he is Mayor of London, they have nothing to fear, and he affectionately hurries them off to the Savoy with Lady Madgy for the secret marriage ceremony. This will be a day of celebration and feasting for all.

Eyre Lady Madgy, Lady Madgy, take two or three of my pie-crust-eaters, my buff-jerkin varlets, that do walk in black gowns at Simon Eyre's heels; take them, good Lady Madgy; trip and go, my brown queen of periwigs, with my delicate Rose and my jolly Rowland to the Savoy; see them linked, countenance the marriage; and when it is done, cling, cling together, you Hamborow turtle-doves. I'll bear you out, come to Simon Eyre; come, dwell with me, Hans, thou shalt eat minced-pies and marchpane. Rose, away, cricket; trip and go, my Lady Madgy, to the Savoy; Hans, wed, and to bed; kiss, and away! Go, vanish! . . . Lord of Ludgate, it's a mad life to be a lord mayor; it's a stirring life, a fine life, a velvet life, a careful life. Well, Simon Eyre, yet set a good face on it, in the honour of Saint Hugh. Soft, the king this day comes to dine with me, to see my new buildings; his majesty is welcome, he shall have good cheer, delicate cheer, princely cheer. This day, my fellow prentices of London come to dine with me too; they shall have fine cheer, gentlemanlike cheer. I promised the mad Cappadocians, when we all served at the Conduit together, that if ever I came to be mayor of London, I would feast them all, and I'll do't, I'll do't, by the life of Pharaoh; by this beard, Sim Eyre will be no flincher. Besides, I have procured that upon every Shrove Tuesday, at the sound of the pancake bell, my fine dapper Assyrian lads shall clap up their shop windows, and away. This is the day, and this day they shall do't, they shall do't.

Boys, that day are you free, let masters care,
And prentices shall pray for Simon Eyre. (*Exit.*)

---

marchpane: marzipan
mad Cappadochians: madcaps
Conduit: it was the custom for London apprentices to carry water to their masters'
houses from the Thames or the water conduits
Shrove Tuesday: the particular holiday of apprentices

Antonio from *Antonio's Revenge* by John Marston

This 'revenge tragedy', written at the turn of the seventeenth century, is set in Italy and is the brutal sequel to Marston's 'satiric romance', *Antonio and Mellida*. Something of a 'bad boy' of his day, Marston uses sensational theatrical techniques, blood and guts to engage his audience.

The son of Andrugio, Duke of Genoa, Antonio is engaged to Mellida, daughter of sadistic tyrant, Piero Sforza, Duke of Venice. In the prequel, Piero defeats the Genoese in battle, but Andrugio and Antonio escape and Piero puts a reward on their heads. Andrugio gives himself up, bringing Antonio to Piero's court in a coffin. Piero appears impressed by Andrugio's courage and the dukes are reunited, whereupon Antonio rises from the coffin to claim Mellida as his bride. Piero agrees to their marriage and the play ends with great rejoicing.

At the beginning of the sequel, Piero's villainous nature is revealed and we see him conspiring to dishonour his daughter to stop the marriage taking place. He plans to poison Andrugio, butcher Antonio and marry his mother . . .

In this scene it is Antonio and Mellida's wedding morning. Antonio has risen at dawn. Gentlemen of his court are joking with him in cheerful mood, but Antonio is full of foreboding and irritated by their trivialities. He tells them about a nightmare he has just had in which two ghosts have appeared – one, murdered and bloody, the other, his father, both demanding revenge. It is horribly prescient of things to come. He recounts how he broke out of the dream and opened his window on to a night sky full of evil portent, still unable to shake off his disturbing nightmare.

Describing the grotesque and distorted dimensions of a dream, the speech is written in iambic pentameter and the language has the dimensions of gothic horror.

When Antonio goes to wake Mellida, the butchered body of Feliche, a Venetian gentleman Piero has implicated in fornication with her, is hung at her window, fulfilling the portents of the dream and spurring Antonio towards revenge.

Antonio

Blow hence these sapless jests. I tell you bloods
My spirit's heavy, and the juice of life
Creeps slowly through my stiffened arteries.
Last sleep my sense was steeped in horrid dreams:
Three parts of night were swallowed in the gulf
Of ravenous time when to my slumbr'ing powers
Two meager ghosts made apparition.
The one's breast seemed fresh-paunched with bleeding wounds
Whose bubbling gore sprang in frighted eye:
The other ghost assumed my father's shape;
Both cried, 'Revenge!' At which my trembling joints
(Icèd quite over with a frozed cold sweat)
Leaped forth the sheets. Three times I gasped at shades,
And thrice, deluded by erroneous sense,
I forced my thoughts make stand; when, lo, I oped
A large bay window, through which the night
Struck terror to my soul. The verge of heaven
Was ringed with flames and all the upper vault
Thick-laced with flakes of fire; in midst whereof
A blazing comet shot his threat'ning train
Just on my face. Viewing these prodigies,
I bowed my naked knee and pierced the star
With an outfacing eye, pronouncing thus:
Deus imperat astris. At which my nose straight bled!
Then doubled I my word, so slunk to bed.

---

sapless jests: stupid jokes
bloods: gentlemen
two meager ghosts: Feliche and Antonio's father, Andrugio
fresh-paunched: newly pierced
I forced my thoughts make stand: pulled myself together
blazing comet: an evil omen
Deus imperat astris: God rules the stars. Antonio is trying to dispel the notion that the portents are evil
my nose straight bled: another evil omen
doubled I my word: I repeated it

Mendoza from *The Malcontent* by John Marston

This dark satire set in Renaissance Genoa was originally performed in 1603 and was hugely popular in its day. It is a complexly plotted commentary on social decadence, steeped in the conventions of the period – intrigue, betrayal, murder, mayhem and disguise – in which Duke Giovanni Altofronto, the deposed Duke of Genoa, returns to his former court disguised as Malvole – the malcontent of the title – to regain his position as rightful ruler. Under cover of madness he delivers home truths, derides court behaviour and exposes adulterous intrigues until finally, righting all wrongs, he regains his kingdom and purges Genoa of his enemies.

Mendoza is courtier to Pietro Janamo, the usurping duke, whom he is cuckolding with his wife Auralia. He is an out-and-out villain, a suave, silver-tongued, callous, voluptuous, mendacious, resourceful and self-regarding man who plots murder, persuades others to kill and is prepared to forfeit all morality in pursuit of his ambitions and to maintain his position.

'Mad' Malvole has just accused Mendoza of being the 'filthy, incontinent fleshmonger' he is, but Mendoza arrogantly dismisses him, confident in his inviolable position at court. Now, alone and 'drunk with favour', he luxuriates in the almost orgasmic benefits it affords. In an evocative description, you can almost hear the buzz and hum of court life, with his onomatopoeic description and hard-edged imagery. The speech is littered with 'O's, lavish superlatives and comparisons with heavenly delights as he indulges in a litany of the benefits of a favoured courtier's life. Respect, subservience, access to the attentions of beautiful women, the 'unutterable pleasures' of sex and the enjoyment of the duchess herself are all described with luxuriating relish. This position at court is what drives him, and when it is threatened there is no bottom to the depths of malice and revenge to which he will stoop in order to restore it.

Mendoza Now, good Elysium! What a delicious Heaven is it for a man to be in a prince's favour! O sweet God! O pleasure! O fortune! O all thou best of life! What should I think, what say, what do? To be a favourite, a minion! To have a general timorous respect observe a man, a stateful silence in his presence, solitariness in his absence, a confused hum and busy murmur of obsequious suitors training him; the cloth held up, the way proclaimed before him; petitionary vassals licking the pavement with their slavish knees, whilst some odd palace-lamprels that engender with snakes, and are full of eyes on both sides, with a kind of insinuated humbleness, fix all their delights upon his brow. O blessed state! What a ravishing prospect doth the Olympus of favour yield! Death, I cornute the duke! Sweet woman, most sweet ladies; nay, angels! By Heaven, he is more accursed than a devil that hates you, or is hated by you, and happier than a god that loves you, or is beloved by you! You preservers of mankind, life-blood of society, who would live, nay, who can live without you? O paradise, how majestical is your austerer presence, how imperiously chaste is your more modest face! But, oh, how full of ravishing attraction is your pretty, petulant, languishing, lasciviously-composed countenance! These amorous smiles, those soul-warming, sparkling glances, ardent as those flames that singed the world by heedless Phaeton! In body how delicate, in soul how witty, in discourse how pregnant, in life how wary, in favours, how judicious, in day how sociable, and in night how – O pleasure unutterable! Indeed, it is most certain, one man cannot deserve only to enjoy a beauteous woman; but a duchess! In despite of Phoebus, I'll write a sonnet instantly in praise of her.

Elysium: the place assigned to the blessed after death in Greek mythology
minion: favourite
training: following
lamprels: lampreys, fishlike creatures that attach themselves by suckers to stones
Olympus: Mount Olympus, home of the Greek gods
cornute: cuckolded
Phaeton: son of Helios, famous for his unlucky driving of the sun chariot
Phoebus: the sun god

Cocledemoy from *The Dutch Courtesan* by John Marston

This comedy – written in 1605 – was reportedly first performed before the court of James I in 1613. In Marston's own words – 'the difference between the love of a courtesan and the wife is the full scope of the play [sexual pun intended], which intermixed with the deceits of a witty city jester fills up the comedy'. It is a tale of virgins and whores, love and lust, double-dealing, trickery and disguise, moving between the lower and upper stratas of society in the vibrant cityscape of an increasingly commercial Jacobean London.

The main plot centres on two friends, noblemen Malheureux and Freevill – their names apt to their natures – who fall under the seductive influence of Franceschina, the Dutch courtesan of the title. A comic sub-plot charts the intrigues of a conman, Cocledemoy, to expose and punish the pretensions of the swindling 'puritanical' publican Mulligrub.

Cocledemoy is a happy-go-lucky city gentleman, a free spirit and something of a force of nature. (His name is thought to derive from that of a coin, but a saucy pun is no doubt intended.) He is a lovable rogue – a thief, a master of disguise, ingenious, indefatigable, capricious, anarchic, wonderfully obscene, bawdy, clever, charming and elusive – 'a man of much money, some wit and less honesty' who doesn't have to earn a living so steals for the sheer hell of it. A challenge to all the norms of acceptable behaviour, he lives by his own rules and administers his own rough justice against the pretensions and hypocrisy of bourgeois society.

In this scene he has been accused by an old whore, Mary Faugh, of 'railing' at her and calling her 'ungodly names' – which indeed he has been, but with such charm and in the most colourful language that he can readily be forgiven. Cocledemoy responds by leaping to his own defence and the defence of the 'oldest' profession, and Mary is visibly flattered as he warms to his theme.

Cocledemoy flags up this eloquent 'pronouncement' as an 'oration', which rather sets the tone. He characterises prostitution as being the most honourable and necessary of all trades – placing it above the twelve legitimate London trade companies – good for commerce and offering a valued commodity to the nobility and the professions. It is a witty and elegantly argued case for an alternative morality.

_____

Cocledemoy Hang toasts! I rail at thee, my worshipful organ-
bellows that fills the pipes, my fine rattling, phlegmy cough o' the
lungs and cold with a pox? I rail at thee? What, my right precious
pandress, supportress of barber-surgeons and enhanceress of lotium
and diet-drink! I rail at thee, necessary damnation? I'll make an
oration, I, in praise of thy most courtly-in-fashion and most
pleasurable function . . . List, then: a bawd, first for her profession
or vocation, it is most worshipful of all the twelve companies; for as
that trade is most honorable that sells the best commodities – as the
draper is more worshipful than the pointmaker, the silkman more
worshipful than the draper, and the goldsmith more honorable
than both, little Mary – so the bawd above all. Her shop has the best
ware; for where these sell but cloth, satins, and jewels, she sells
divine virtues as virginity, modesty, and such rare gems, and those
not like a petty chapman, by retail, but like a great merchant, by
wholesale. Wa, ha, ho! And who are her customers? Not base corn-
cutters or sowgelders, but most rare wealthy knights and most rare
bountiful lords are her customers. Again, whereas no trade or
vocation profiteth but by the loss and displeasure of another – as
the merchant thrives not but by the licentiousness of giddy and
unsettled youth, the lawyer but by the vexation of his client, the
physician but by the maladies of his patient – only my smooth-
gumm'd bawd lives by others' pleasure, and only grows rich by
others' rising. O merciful gain! O righteous income! So much for her
vocation, trade, and life. As for their death, how can it be bad since
their wickedness is always before their eyes, and a death's head most
commonly on their middle finger? To conclude, 'tis most certain
they must needs both live well and die well since most commonly
they live in Clerkenwell and die in Bridewell. *Dixi*, Mary.

Hang toasts: Cocledemoy's favourite expression. Spiced toasts soaked in liquor were a
popular treat of the day
phlegmy: watery
pox: syphilis
barber-surgeons: these two professions operated under one guild
enhanceress: someone who 'enhances' the price of something
lotium: stale urine used by barbers to flatten the hair
diet-drink: treatment for the pox
twelve companies: the twelve trade guilds

pointmaker: lacemaker
petty chapman: retailer
Wa, ha, ho!: the cry the falconer makes to lure the falcon
corn-cutters: chiropodists
smooth-gummed: having no teeth
death's head: a ring with a skull commonly worn by procuresses
Clerkenwell: haunt for thieves and prostitutes
Bridewell: prison
Dixi: Latin for 'I have spoken', a Roman pronouncement of judgement

Volpone from *Volpone* by Ben Jonson

First performed in 1605, *Volpone* is appropriately set in
Venice, considered to be the throbbing heart of opulence
and debauchery in the seventeenth century, and is a satire
on greed and lust in a money-obsessed society.

A rich and childless nobleman, Volpone, and his
parasitic lackey, Mosca, conspire to swindle three avaricious
bounty hunters, each of whom wants to be Volpone's sole
heir. In a well-planned scam, Volpone pretends to be on his
deathbed so they will shower him with expensive presents
to win his favour and, subsequently, his ill-gotten fortune.

Celia, the virtuous young wife of the bounty hunter
Corvino, has been described by Mosca as one of the most
beautiful women in Italy. Her jealous husband keeps her
guarded under lock and key, but inflamed by Mosca's
luminous description, and a brief sighting, Volpone
determines to have her by any means. Mosca convinces
Corvino that if he allows Celia to lie next to the dying man,
it will encourage Volpone to name him as sole heir and
probably bring about his early death. Corvino is persuaded
and Celia is dragged into Volpone's sickroom. The moment
she is left alone Volpone leaps from his 'deathbed' and
makes his play.

Jonson's characters are 'types' that his audiences could
recognise – Mosca the fly, Corvino the raven, and Celia,
whose name derives from the Latin *caelum*, meaning 'sky' or
'heaven'. Volpone is a sly fox. He is rapacious, hedonistic,
covetous, sadistic, lecherous, greedy for money and self-
gratification and crafty as his namesake. Driven by his
feverish lust for Celia, who is now at his mercy, he forces his
attentions on her. In language rich with seductive and poetic
imagery, he tempts her with promises of extraordinary
pleasures, presenting himself with this 'foreplay' of titillating
verbal pyrotechnics as a potent godlike lover. He is a
dangerous powerhouse of sexual energy, and will not be
thwarted (note the implicit warning in the first line of the
speech). Celia must submit or be taken.

Volpone

If thou hast wisdom, hear me, Celia.
Thy baths shall be the juice of July-flowers,
Spirit of roses, and of violets,
The milk of unicorns, and panthers' breath
Gathered in bags and mixed with Cretan wines.
Our drink shall be preparèd gold and amber,
Which we will take until my roof whirl round
With the vertigo; and my dwarf shall dance,
My eunuch sing, my fool make up the antic.
Whilst we, in changèd shapes, act Ovid's tales,
Thou like Europa now, and I like Jove,
Then I like Mars, and thou like Erycine;
So of the rest, till we have quite run through,
And wearied all the fables of the gods.
Then will I have thee in more modern forms,
Attirèd like some sprightly dame of France,
Brave Tuscan lady, or proud Spanish beauty;
Sometimes unto the Persian Sophy's wife,
Or the Grand Signior's mistress; and, for change,
To one of our most artful courtesans,
Or some quick Negro, or cold Russian;
And I will meet thee in as many shapes;
Where we may so transfuse our wand'ring souls
Out at our lips and score up sums of pleasures,
        That the curious shall not know
          How to tell them as they flow;
        And the envious, when they find
          What their number is, be pined.

Husband from *A Yorkshire Tragedy* (anon)

This one-act domestic tragedy was first published in 1608 and attributed to Shakespeare, but probably a dishonest publisher made the unlikely attribution in order to sell more copies.

The play is based on a true story of the day. A rich Yorkshire landowner, Walter Claverley, facing ruin as a result of gambling debts and a dissolute lifestyle, attempted to murder his wife, killed two of his children and was on his way to kill a third when he was caught and executed.

In this scene the Master of an Oxford college visits the Husband to tell him his brother, a promising theology student, has taken responsibility for his debts and is in prison, thus scuppering a brilliant future. He begs the Husband to pay off the debts and save him. Pushed into a corner, the Husband undertakes to resolve the matter, knowing he has no means to do so. Forced into a realisation of what he has done, he laments his profligacy and the damage he has caused.

The 'lament' or soliloquy is a common set piece in Elizabethan drama, a device designed to give the audience an insight into a character's thought processes. In this speech we are given access to the Husband's confusion and torment. His downfall has been women, wine and gambling. He berates Heaven for putting such temptations in his path when they only lead to misery. It is a man's natural disposition to eat forbidden fruits, he argues, so why does God allow them? He harangues himself with questions, yet he knows full well that he is the architect of his own misery. He has lost everything – his reputation, land and a fortune that has been in his family for generations. Look how he repeats 'generations, generations' in a groan of acknowledgement. He knows there is no hope of redeeming his brother and that he will bring down his family with him. Prosperity and promise has been turned to disgrace and ruin. Seeing no solution and no prospect of escape, the scene is set for him to kill his children rather than see them face disgrace and starvation.

Husband   Oh thou confused man! Thy pleasant sins have undone thee, thy damnation has beggared thee. That Heaven should say we must not sin and yet made women; gives our senses way to find pleasure which being found confounds us! Why should we know those things so much misuse us? Oh, would virtue had been forbidden; we should then have proved all virtuous, for 'tis our blood to love what we are forbidden. Had not drunkenness been forbidden what man would have been fool to a beast and zany to a swine, to show tricks in the mire? What is there in three dice to make a man draw thrice three thousand acres into the compass of a round, little table, and with the gentleman's palsy in the hand shake out his posterity thieves or beggars? 'Tis done; I ha' don't i'faith: terrible, horrible misery! How well was I left? Very well, very well. My lands showed like a full moon about me, but now the moon's i'the last quarter, waning, waning; and I am mad to think that moon was mine. Mine and my father's, and my forefathers': generations, generations! Down goes the house of us, down, down it sinks. Now is the name a beggar, begs in me; that name, which hundreds of years has made this shire famous, in me and my posterity runs out. In my seed five are made miserable besides myself: my riot is now my brother's gaoler, my wife's sighing, my three boys' penury, and mine own confusion.
Why sit my hairs upon my cursed head? (*Tears his hair.*)
　Will not this poison scatter them? Oh!
　My brother's in execution among devils
　That stretch him and make him give, and I in want
　Not able to deliver, nor to redeem him.
　Divines and dying men may talk of hell
　But in my heart her several torments dwell.
　Slavery and misery! Who in this case
　Would not take up money upon his soul,
　Pawn his salvation, live at interest?
　I that did ever in abundance dwell,
　For me to want exceeds the throes of hell.

---

fool to: inferior to
zany to: buffooning imitation of

Subtle from *The Alchemist* by Ben Jonson

A satire on gullibility and greed, *The Alchemist* was first performed in 1610. Set in London, in the aftermath of the plague of 1609, it offers fascinating insights into fast-moving city life, its colourful characters of quacks, social climbers and lowlife, and the way in which alchemy was perceived at the beginning of the seventeenth century.

The plot centres on the antics of three con artists: Face, a butler and master of disguise; Dol Common, a prostitute; and Subtle, an alchemist – all aptly named and recognisable stereotypes.

When the plague drives Face's well-heeled master from his house, the formidable triumvirate set up shop in it, with a view to preying on their greedy and gullible customers, using Face's gift of the gab, Dol Common's more womanly 'persuasions' and Subtle's claims to 'amazing' alchemic gifts. Subtle is a confidence trickster who is motivated by delight in gulling his victims. He was a 'no buttocks' pauper before Face met him, but now practises his quackery in the shop.

Here, the scamming trio has been approached by Sir Epicure Mammon, a befuddled bon viveur who has come to avail himself of one of their get-rich-quick schemes. He believes he is buying a philosopher's stone with which to turn all the base-metal objects in his house to gold. He is very excited at the prospect and has brought along his clever and sceptical friend, Pertinax Surly, who remains to be convinced of Subtle's abilities.

Egged on by Mammon, Subtle regales him with this 'sales pitch' for his alchemic arts and an explanation of where gold comes from. It is a discourse designed to deceive and obfuscate, to impress and blind the suspicious Surly with science. What seems to be intelligent analysis is pseudo-learned jargon, littered with improbably scientific concepts and terminology and inappropriate snippets of Latin.

Jonson's blank verse skilfully adapts to suit Subtle's patter – the comedy deriving from his obscure explanations and unedifying logic as to how the science works.

Subtle

It is, of the one part,
A humid exhalation, which we call
Materia liquida, or the unctuous water;
On th' other part, a certain crass and viscous
Portion of earth; both which, concorporate,
Do make the elementary matter of gold;
Which is not yet *propria materia*,
But common to all metals and all stones.
For, where it is forsaken of that moisture,
And hath more dryness, it becomes a stone;
Where it retains more of the humid fatness,
It turns to sulphur or to quicksilver,
Who are the parents of all other metals.
Nor can this remote matter suddenly
Progress so from extreme unto extreme,
As to grow gold, and leap o'er all the means.
Nature doth forst beget th' imperfect, then
Proceeds she to the perfect. Of that airy
And oily water, mercury is engend'red;
Sulphur o' the fat and earthy part; the one
Which is the last supplying the place of male,
The other of the female, in all metals.
Some do believe hermaphrodeity,
That both do act and suffer. But these two
Make the rest ductile, malleable, extensive.
And even in gold they are; for we do find
Seeds of them by our fire, and gold in them;
And can produce the species of each metal
More perfect thence, than nature doth in earth.
Besides, who doth not see in daily practice
Art can beget bees, hornets, beetles, wasps,
Out of the carcasses and dung of creatures;
Yea, scorpions of an herb, being rightly placed?
And these are living creatures, far more perfect
And excellent than metals.

Cardinal Wolsey from *Henry VIII* by William Shakespeare

This history play from 1613 is less frequently performed than many in the Shakespeare canon, being considered of doubtful authenticity and unfairly dismissed as 'pageantry'. Nevertheless, it has some splendid speeches in it.

Katharine of Aragon, Henry VIII's first wife, was originally married to Henry's brother, Arthur – a match arranged to cement an alliance with Spain against France. Arthur died five months later and shortly afterwards she married Henry. Their marriage lasted over twenty years until Henry, desperate for a male heir and infatuated by Katharine's maid of honour, Anne Boleyn, wanted a divorce. Katharine, a devout Catholic, refused to give it to him. Henry sought the support of Cardinal Wolsey to intercede with the Pope.

Thomas Wolsey, a brilliant and ambitious butcher's son, is a commoner who has risen to a position of almost unlimited power during Henry's reign. As both Cardinal and Chancellor, he has held the highest offices in both church and state, but his favour with Henry, his ostentatious lifestyle, greed and blatant corruption have made him deeply unpopular at court, and his split loyalties between Henry and Rome now prove his undoing. Treacherous letters he has written to the Pope about the King's divorce, and inventories of his vast accumulated wealth have fallen into Henry's hands. Betrayed by his closest friend and ally, Henry orders Wolsey to surrender the Great Seal, removes all titles and commands that all his goods and lands be confiscated. Wolsey is a broken old man. He knows what is in store for him. He is saying goodbye to all the 'pomp and glory of the world' and all his influence – realising, too late, with painful resignation, the hollowness of his ambitions, the fickleness of favour and how far he has fallen from the grace of God. He seems to have found a calm accommodation with his fate. The burdens of high office have been set down with some relief and replaced with better hopes of heaven.

Wolsey

So farewell to the little good you bear me.
Farewell, a long farewell, to all my greatness!
This is the state of man: to-day he puts forth
The tender leaves of hopes; to-morrow blossoms
And bears his blushing honours thick upon him;
The third day comes a frost, a killing frost,
And when he thinks, good easy man, full surely
His greatness is a-ripening, nips his root,
And then he falls, as I do. I have ventur'd,
Like little wanton boys that swim on bladders,
This many summers in a sea of glory;
But far beyond my depth. My high-blown pride
At length broke under me, and now has left me,
Weary and old with service, to the mercy
Of a rude stream, that must for ever hide me.
Vain pomp and glory of this world, I hate ye;
I feel my heart new open'd. O, how wretched
Is that poor man that hangs on princes' favours!
There is betwixt that smile we would aspire to,
That sweet aspect of princes, and their ruin
More pangs and fears than wars or women have;
And when he falls, he falls like Lucifer,
Never to hope again.

De Flores from *The Changeling* by Thomas Middleton and William Rowley

The Changeling (one who is not what he or she appears to be) was written in 1622 and is regarded as one of the masterpieces of Jacobean theatre. Set in Catholic Spain, it is a typically gory tragedy about obsessive passion, male domination, murder, revenge and moral decay.

Beatrice-Joanne is the beautiful, spoilt and wholly immoral daughter of the nobleman Vermandero, governor of Alicante. De Flores is his servant, a repulsive fellow who is sexually obsessed with her. Beatrice finds him repugnant and insults him at every opportunity. De Flores knows she hates him but is nevertheless prepared to do anything to possess her, including murder, weathering her scorn just to stay in her sight. He is a foul, unprincipled, dangerous villain driven by sexual appetite – obsequious when it serves his turn, malicious, cunning, lewd and treacherous. The more Beatrice abuses him, the more it hardens his resolve to have her.

In this scene he has sought out Beatrice once again, ostensibly to deliver a message from her father. He watches from a distance as she secretly passes a letter to a friend of Alsemero, the man she loves in spite of being promised by her father to Alonzo, another nobleman. As he watches, De Flores shares his obsession with the audience. It doesn't matter how badly she treats him, he can't help inventing excuses just to see her. He is like a whipped dog that keeps coming back for more in the hope that one day his mistress will stroke him. He acknowledges his ugliness but sees far less appetising specimens being loved, so why not him?

Driven by lust for Alsemero, desperate to be rid of Alonzo yet appear the chaste and dutiful daughter, Beatrice conspires with a willing De Flores to kill him, but after the murder De Flores hides the body and demands her virginity as a reward. Repelled at having placed herself at his mercy and brought herself down to his level she is forced to submit, setting the scene for bloody and fatal consequences.

De Flores (*aside*)   Yonder's she.
Whatever ails me, now o'late especially,
I can as well be hanged as refrain from seeing her;
Some twenty times a day, nay, not so little,
Do I force errands, frame ways and excuses
To come into her sight, and I have small reason for't,
And less encouragement; for she baits me still
Every time worse than other, does profess herself
The cruellest enemy to my face in town,
At no hand can abide the sight of me,
As if danger, or ill luck hung in my looks.
I must confess my face is bad enough,
But I know far worse has better fortune,
And not endured alone, but doted on;
And yet such pick-haired faces, chins like witches',
Here and there five hairs, whispering in a corner,
As if they grew in fear of one another,
Wrinkles like troughs, where swine deformity swills
The tears of perjury that lie there like wash
Fallen from the slimy and dishonest eye, –
Yet such a one plucked sweets without restraint,
And has the grace of beauty to his sweet.
Though my hard fate has thrust me out to servitude,
I tumbled into th'world a gentleman. –
She turns her blessed eye upon me now,
And I'll endure all storms before I part with't.

---

pick-hair'd: sparsely bearded
wash: lotion
sweet: sweetheart

Luke from *The City Madam* by Philip Massinger

Philip Massinger was a contemporary of Shakespeare, writing regularly for the King's Men, the leading theatre company in London, between 1613 and 1640.

A well-observed social satire, *The City Madam* centres on the Frugal family. Luke is the villainous older brother of Sir John, a rich London merchant. As a result of a dissipated and extravagant lifestyle, Luke has ended up in debtors' prison. His brother has redeemed him, clothed him and offered him a roof, and although Sir John's wife and daughters treat him with contempt, Luke responds with servile humility and appears a changed man.

When suitors come to court Sir John's two daughters, Lady Frugal's astronomer tells them that the stars dictate their husbands should be obedient to their every whim. As a result, the girls make such outrageous demands that the suitors decide not to marry them after all. They report the girls' behaviour to Sir John who decides to teach his wife and daughters a lesson in humility, and test his brother's sincerity. He lets it be known he has retired to a French monastery, leaving the care of his family and administration of his fortune in Luke's hands.

Here, Luke has just discovered his good luck. Rhapsodising over his newly acquired and unexpected wealth, his earlier subservience is a thing of the past. He has the key to Sir John's counting house in his hand – the 'dumb magician', 'a mistress to be hugged over' that has opened the door to untold riches.

The soliloquy is essentially about greed. Luke is metaphorically rubbing his hands together, salivating at the opulence of it all. Observe the line endings and the energy and stresses of each line and you will be able to navigate your way through the succulent imagery and convey Luke's mouth-watering relish at the contents of the vault. Towards the end of the speech we learn that Luke intends to call in all debts owing to his brother to line his own pockets even more. He feels transported out of this world by the prospect.

By the end of the play he will have resorted to the vilest extortion and betrayed the women in his care. But Sir John has a surprise in store. A trap has been laid that will flush out Luke's villainy and deliver a fantastic piece of justice.

Luke

'Twas no fantastic object, but a truth,
A real truth. Nor dream: I did not slumber,
And could wake ever with a brooding eye
To gaze upon't! It did endure the touch;
I saw, and felt it. Yet what I beheld
And handl'd oft, did so transcend belief
(My wonder and astonishment pass'd o'er),
I faintly could give credit to my senses.
Thou dumb magician, that without a charm
Did'st make my entrance easy, to possess
What wise men wish, and toil for. Hermes' moly,
Sibylla's golden bough, the great elixir,
Imagin'd only by the alchemist,
Compar'd with thee are shadows; thou the substance
And guardian of felicity. No marvel
My brother made thy place of rest his bosom,
Thou being the keeper of his heart, a mistress
To be hugg'd ever. In by-corners of
This sacred room, silver in bags heap'd up
Like billets saw'd, and ready for the fire,
Unworthy to hold fellowship with bright gold
That flow'd about the room, conceal'd itself.
There needs no artificial light; the splendour
Makes a perpetual day there, night and darkness
By that still-burning lamp for ever banish'd.
But when, guided by that, my eyes had made
Discovery of the caskets, and they open'd,
Each sparkling diamond from itself shot forth
A pyramid of flames, and in the roof
Fix'd it, a glorious star, and made the place
Heaven's abstract, or epitome. Rubies, sapphires,
And ropes of orient pearl, these seen, I could not
But look on with contempt. And yet I found
What weak credulity could have no faith in,
A treasure far exceeding these. Here lay

A manor bound fast in a skin of parchment,
The wax continuing hard, the acres melting.
Here a sure deed of gift for a market town,
If not redeem'd this day, which is not in
The unthrift's power: there being scarce one shire
In Wales or England, where my moneys are not
Lent out at usury, the certain hook
To draw in more. I am sublim'd! Gross earth
Supports me not. I walk on air!

Hermes' moly: the magic flower Hermes gave to Ulysses to protect him from the sorceress, Circe, who had the power to turn folk into beasts
Sibylla's golden bough: the golden bough that the Sibyl of Cumae instructed him to pluck to see him safely through the underworld
the great elixir: when ground up and boiled in water, the philosopher's stone turned base metals into gold

Giovanni from *'Tis Pity She's a Whore* by John Ford

Ford's reputation rests largely on this play. It was first published in 1633, but because of its affinity to Jacobean revenge tragedies like *The Duchess of Malfi*, some think it was written much earlier. Set in Parma, in the bustling domestic environment of mercantile society, it addresses themes of lust, vengeance, greed and the controversial issue of incestuous love that finally pulls everyone's world apart.

In this scene at the beginning of the play, Giovanni, a brilliant, rebellious young student, has returned home from his studies at Bologna University, accompanied by his tutor, Friar Bonaventura. Fuelled by desire for his beautiful sister Annabella (the 'whore' of the title), he tells the friar about his feelings. They are so intense, he must share them with someone, or burst. The older man is naturally horrified and makes his position clear. But Giovanni is so driven by his passion he seems blind to all moral or Christian argument, and he makes a powerful case against moral norms and for flouting convention. While he addresses the question, almost as a matter for academic debate, he is in torment. Torn between public morality and personal desire, he seeks the approval of his mentor to go down the path he feels he is driven by fate to follow. His passion seems to have a life of its own – 'It were more ease to stop the ocean . . . than to dissuade by vows' – and he can't resist it. He sees no option but to follow it, knowing it must inevitably end in ruin.

The distraught Giovanni goes to Annabella to tell her of his feelings which she reciprocates and they consummate their love. But when Annabella becomes pregnant, she is forced to marry a rich nobleman to conceal her guilt, but her husband discovers her secret and plots to kill Giovanni. Annabella tries to warn him, but mad with jealousy he accuses her of inconstancy and stabs her to death. He appears at her husband's banquet with her heart impaled on his dagger before he himself is killed in a scene worthy of the last act of *Hamlet*.

Giovanni Gentle father,
   To you I have unclasped my burdened soul,
   Emptied the storehouse of my thoughts and heart,
   Made myself poor of secrets; have not left
   Another word untold, which hath not spoke
   All what I ever durst, or think, or know;
   And yet is here the comfort I shall have,
   Must I not do what all men else may, love?
   Must I not praise
   That beauty which, if framed anew, the gods
   Would make a god of, if they had it there,
   And kneel to it, as I do kneel to them?
   Shall a peevish sound,
   A customary form, from man to man,
   Of brother and of sister, be a bar
   'Twixt my perpetual happiness and me?
   Say that we had one father, say one womb
   (Curse to my joys) gave both us life and birth;
   Are we not therefore each to other bound
   So much the more by nature? by the links
   Of blood, of reason? nay, if you will have't,
   Even of religion, to be ever one,
   One soul, one flesh, one love, one heart, one all?
   Shall then, for that I am her brother born,
   My joys be ever banished from her bed?
   No, father; in your eyes I see the change
   Of pity and compassion; from your age,
   As from a sacred oracle, distils
   The life of counsel: tell me, holy man,
   What cure shall give me case in these extremes.

---

peevish: trifling
customary form: convention

Willmore from *The Rover* by Aphra Behn

Aphra Behn was probably the first woman to make a living as a writer. Her best-known play, *The Rover*, first performed in 1677, is a feisty comedy of intrigue about sexual politics, the role of women in Restoration society and the adventures of a roving band of Englishmen who fetch up in Naples to enjoy the carnival.

Willmore (the Rover of the title) is an impoverished sea captain, exiled as a result of his support for Charles II during the rule of Oliver Cromwell. He is a charming and handsome young rake who lusts after every beautiful young woman he sees. In the previous scene he has seen pictures of Angellica Bianca, a much sought-after courtesan, hung in front of her house to advertise her wares. Willmore is immediately smitten and curses his poverty – at a thousand crowns a month she is well beyond his means. Unable to resist, he takes a picture, angering his companions by the 'insult'. A fight ensues but Angellica, overhearing, intervenes. The silver-tongued Willmore argues that as he cannot afford Angellica's price, he wants her picture as a poor substitute. Angellica, falling under the spell of his charm, allows him to keep it.

In this scene, Angellica summons him to her chamber under the pretext of seeking an apology. A sparring dialogue ensues in which Willmore enquires how much of her time his limited resources can buy. Angellica affects outrage and taunts him with poverty.

Willmore is a typical Restoration libertine with a terrific sexual appetite. 'A power too strong to be resisted' and, as his name implies, 'always wanting more'. This speech, written in loose blank verse, has a rather 'elevated' tone as Willmore pretends to stand on his dignity as a gentleman, balancing his 'contempt' for Angellica's trade with a willingness to sacrifice his last penny to have her. A seductive performance, it primes Angellica to break the rules of her trade and offer him her love in return for his own, and the lecherous Willmore is happy to comply in order to achieve another conquest.

Willmore

Yes, I am poor; but I'm a gentleman,
And one that scorns this baseness which you practise.
Poor as I am, I would not sell myself,
No, not to gain your charming high-prized person.
Though I admire you strangely for your beauty,
Yet I contemn your mind.
And yet I would at any rate enjoy you,
At your own rate, but cannot: see here
The only sum I can command on earth;
I know not where to eat when this is gone.
Yet such a slave I am to love and beauty,
This last reserve I'll sacrifice to enjoy you.
Nay, do not frown, I know you're to be bought,
And would be bought by me, by me,
For a mean trifling sum, if I could pay it down:
Which happy knowledge I will still repeat,
And lay it to my heart; it has a virtue in't,
And soon will cure those wounds your eyes have made.
And yet, there's something so divinely powerful there –
Nay, I will gaze, to let you see my strength.
(*Holds her, looks on her, and pauses and sighs.*)
By heaven, bright creature, I would not for the world
Thy fame were half so fair as is thy face.
(*Turns her away from him.*)
Yes; you shall hear how infamous you are,
For which I do not hate thee,
But that secures my heart, and all the flames it feels
Are but so many lusts;
I know it by their sudden bold intrusion.
The fire's impatient and betrays; 'tis false:
For had it been the purer flame of love,
I should have pined and languished at your feet,
Ere found the impudence to have discovered it.
I now dare stand your scorn, and your denial.

Serapion from *All for Love, or A World Well Lost* by John Dryden

John Dryden, Poet Laureate to Charles II and James II, was one of the great literary figures of the late seventeenth century. *All for Love*, first performed in 1678, is his retelling of Shakespeare's *Antony and Cleopatra*. Written in blank verse in acknowledged imitation of Shakespeare, it is considered Dryden's greatest play. The action takes place during the lovers' last hours in a single location outside the temple of Isis in Alexandria, while Roman armies mass in the hills above the city threatening Egypt. It explores the moral and intellectual conflict between public duty and private passion resulting from the couple's adultery.

Roman military commander, Mark Antony, has fallen under the spell of Cleopatra, the beautiful and voluptuous Queen of Egypt, for whom he has abandoned his duty to both wife and country. Holed up in the temple in a state of conflict and suicidal despair, he fears he has lost Cleopatra to the Roman Emperor, Caesar, while former allies are now his enemies. He has not seen his lover for several days and concerns are growing that Egypt will be doomed without Antony's allegiance. Everything is in the balance because of Cleopatra.

Serapion is a priest in the temple of the goddess Isis – an important figure in Egyptian society. The Egyptians believe the gods spoke to them through their priests in signs and omens, so his words carry great weight and significance.

In this speech – at the start of the play – he describes a catalogue of fearful portents he has witnessed to some other priests. It is for their ears only. He is aware of the demoralising effect such portents would have on the Egyptian armies. These are portents of almost biblical proportions – the unnatural flooding of the Nile, sea creatures stranded and thrashing in the mud and a vision of the dead bursting from their graves to prophesy the end of Egypt are described in terrifying and graphic detail. Written in splendidly muscular poetry, the speech acts as a prologue, setting the scene and presaging the tragic events that are to come.

Serapion

Portents and prodigies have grown so frequent,
That they have lost their name. Our fruitful Nile
Flowed ere the wonted season, with a torrent
So unexpected, and so wondrous fierce,
That the wild deluge overtook the haste
Even of the hinds that watched it: Men and beasts
Were borne above the tops of trees, that grew
On the utmost margin of the water-mark.
Then, with so swift an ebb the flood drove backward,
It slipt from underneath the scaly herd:
Here monstrous phocæ panted on the shore;
Forsaken dolphins there with their broad tails,
Lay lashing the departing waves: hard by them,
Sea horses floundering in the slimy mud,
Tossed up their heads, and dashed the ooze about them.
Last night, between the hours of twelve and one,
In a lone aisle of the temple while I walked,
A whirlwind rose, that, with a violent blast,
Shook all the dome: the doors around me clapt;
The iron wicket, that defends the vault,
Where the long race of Ptolemies is laid,
Burst open, and disclosed the mighty dead.
From out each monument, in order placed,
An armed ghost starts up: the boy-king last
Reared his inglorious head. A peal of groans
Then followed, and a lamentable voice
Cried, Egypt is no more! My blood ran back,
My shaking knees against each other knocked;
On the cold pavement down I fell entranced,
And so unfinished left the horrid scene.

Scaramouch from *The Emperor of the Moon* by Aphra Behn

First performed in 1687, this is a dazzling pantomime *commedia dell'arte* farce involving deception, music, flying machines, illusions, disguises and visual effects.

The plot centres on Dr Baliardo and his obsession with inhabitants on the moon. So absorbed is he with his alternative reality that he thwarts the wedding plans of his daughter Elaria to keep her available for marriage to the Emperor of the Moon. Elaria and her cousin Bellemante (also denied her choice of husband) are forced to play him at his own game, so they employ two servants, Scaramouch (Baliardo's man) and Harlequin, to trick the doctor into agreeing to the weddings of their choice. They use a number of ludicrous strategies to save the day, which culminate in the girls' lovers fooling Baliardo into believing they are the Emperor of the Moon and the Prince of Thunderland. It is only after the couples are married that Baliardo discovers his mistake and how foolish he has been.

Scaramouch (stock character from the *commedia dell'arte*) is an unscrupulous, artful manservant, and his affinity for intrigue often lands him in difficult situations – from which he always manages to escape. He is in love with Mopsophil, governess to Elaria and Bellemante, and in competition with Harlequin for her favours. In this scene he is disguised as an apothecary so he can secretly deliver love letters to Elaria and Bellemante from their suitors, and press his own suit with Mopsophil at the same time.

In the first section of the speech he relishes the cleverness of his strategy. But when his employer arrives on the scene, the disguise is really tested. He launches into a pretentious diatribe, playing up to Baliardo's vanity and scientific obsessions. His master is completely taken in and much impressed by Scaramouch's seeming erudition, which spurs him on. Always with an eye to the main chance, he seizes the moment to enlist Baliardo's support for his pursuit of Mopsophil and gain an advantage over his rival.

Scaramouch   The devil's in't, if either the doctor, my master, or Mopsophil, know me in this disguise; and thus, I may not only gain my mistress, and out-wit Harlequin, but deliver the ladies those letters from their lovers, which I took out of his pocket this morning; and who would suspect an apothecary for a pimp? Nor can the jade Mopsophil, in honour, refuse a person of my gravity, and (*pointing to his shop*) so well set up. Hum, the doctor here first; this is not so well, but I'm prepared with impudence for all encounters.

(*Enter the* **Doctor**. **Scaramouch** *salutes him gravely*.)

– Most reverend Doctor Baliardo. (*Bows*.) I might, through great pusillanimity, blush to give you this anxiety, did I not opine you were as gracious as communitive and eminent; and though you have no cognizance of me, your humble servant, yet I have of you, you being so greatly famed for your admirable skill, both in Galenical and Paracelsian phenomenas, and other approved felicities in vulnerary emetics, and purgative experiences. And though I am at present busied in writing (those few observations I have accumulated in my peregrinations, sir), yet the ambition I aspired to, of being an ocular and aurial witness of your singularity, made me trespass on your sublimer affairs. Besides a violent inclination, sir, of being initiated into the denomination of your learned family, by the conjugal circumference of a matrimonial tie, with that singularly accomplished person, madam the governante of your hostel. And, if I may obtain your condescension to my hymenaeal propositions, I doubt not my operation with the fair one.

---

communitive: belonging to the community, full of good fellowship
Galenical and Paracelsian: Galen and Paracelsus were both famous medical practitioners
aurial: by the ear
Governante of your hostel: governess of your residence = Mopsophil
hymeaeal: pertaining to marriage
condescention: agreement
operation with: influence on

Jeremy Fetch from *Love for Love* by William Congreve

This wonderful comedy of manners was first performed in 1695. In a masterful plot, rich with social observation and witty dialogue, Congreve addresses the themes of love, money, hypocrisy, inheritance, growing old and the timeless conflict between parent and offspring.

The play begins in the chambers of Valentine, a young rake, who has spent all his money on high living and the fruitless pursuit of the lovely heiress Angelica. He is lying low to escape his creditors, poring haplessly over books of philosophy. He determines to write a play and court his beloved with philosophy and poetry. He plans to woo her with wit and engage her compassion with his poverty.

Jeremy Fetch (fetch by name and fetch by nature) is Valentine's good-humoured, quick-witted and faithful servant who is sufficiently trusted and relied on to be able to speak his mind. Jeremy will die, starve or be damned with his master, but the prospect of his literary pursuits is a bridge too far. Unimpressed by these literary ambitions, he 'dismisses his master from any future authority over him'. But Valentine has other plans, clearly expecting Jeremy to act as his researcher in the art of writing poetry. If there is any work to be done, Jeremy must do it!

Horrified by his master's intentions, Jeremy makes his position crystal clear. He knows Valentine is out of favour with his father because of his debts and idling, and can't fathom how his latest obsession will endear him, especially if his hard-working seaman brother comes home. How can he pay his debts with poetry? What woman would not prefer a rich idiot to a witty poet with no fortune? He has his master's best interests at heart and makes a compelling argument to dissuade him from his course – debunking wit and poetry, denouncing his literary haunts as being more decadent than gambling and the races, and painting the most pejorative picture of poets and their ilk. A real sense of Valentine's playboy pursuits and lifestyle is revealed with Jeremy's ripe and unfavourable comparisons.

Jeremy But sir, is this the way to recover your father's favour? Why, Sir Sampson will be irreconcilable. If your younger brother should come from sea, he'd never look upon you again. You're undone, sir, you're ruined; you won't have a friend left in the world if you turn poet. Ah, pox confound that Will's coffee-house, it has ruined more young men than the Royal Oak Lottery. Nothing thrives that belongs to't. The man of the house would have been an alderman by this time with half the trade, if he had set up in the city. For my part, I never sit at the door that I don't get double the stomach that I do at a horse-race. The air upon Banstead-Downs is nothing to it for a whetter. Yet I never see it but the spirit of famine appears to me; sometimes like a decayed porter, worn out with pimping and carrying *billet-doux* and songs, not like other porters for hire, but for the jest's sake; now like a thin chairman, melted down to half his proportion with carrying a poet upon tick to visit some great fortune, and his fare to be paid him like the wages of sin, either at the day of marriage, or the day of death. Sometimes like a bilked bookseller, with a meagre terrified countenance, that looks as if he had written for himself, or were resolved to turn author and bring the rest of his brethren into the same condition; and lastly, in the form of a worn-out punk, with verses in her hand, which her vanity had preferred to settlements, without a whole tatter to her tail, but as ragged as one of the muses, or as if she were carrying her linen to the paper-mill, to be converted into folio books of warning to all young maids not to prefer poetry to good sense, or lying in the arms of a needy wit before the embraces of a wealthy fool.

Will's coffee-house: the poet Dryden's drinking den, named after its owner, Will Urwin
Royal Oak Lottery: an annual lottery
Banstead-Downs: Epsom Downs
get double the stomach: want to drink twice as much
whetter: one whose appetite is stimulated for more
chairman: sedan carrier
bilked: cheated
punk: whore

Faulkland from *The Rivals* by Richard Brinsley Sheridan

One of the most hilarious of late-Restoration comedies, *The Rivals* was first performed in 1775. Set in the spa town of Bath, a fashionable resort for the aspiring middle classes and aristocracy of eighteenth-century England, it is a skilful mix of social satire, sophisticated wit, plot and subplot that snipes at love, marriage, class and wealth.

Fed on a diet of lurid romantic fiction, young and beautiful Lydia Languish concludes that the only way to ensure true love is to eschew her riches and marry a poor man. To win her hand, dashing Captain Jack Absolute, wealthy son of a baronet, Sir Anthony, poses as Ensign Beverley – the impecunious lover of her fantasies. Meanwhile, Sir Anthony is trying to arrange Jack's marriage to Lydia through her guardian, the language-mangling Mrs Malaprop, and in consequence, Jack becomes a rival to himself.

Simultaneously, Jack's friend, Faulkland, has fallen in love with Sir Anthony's ward, Julia. Although his love is returned, Faulkland is consumed with jealousy and doubt, driving him to submit Julia to numerous validations of her love. These she has tolerated with some distress, attributing his behaviour to an excess of humility and lack of self-worth.

Here, in desperation, finally, Julia offers a trial separation to prove her fidelity, but Faulkland reads this as a desire to be free of him. Julia exits in tears and Faulkland stands outside her door, racked by remorse.

Faulkland is the archetypal sentimental hero plagued by an irrational and impossible ideal of love. He knows how badly he behaves, but he is a slave to his unfounded jealous imaginings – more preoccupied with being loved than loving. It is a self-destructive streak that is ruining the very thing he wants most. The speech, littered with exclamation marks, uses the ridiculously overblown language of high romance. Although Faulkland's suffering is real and should be played truthfully, the comedy derives from Sheridan's parody of a besotted hero.

Faulkland I do not mean to distress you. – If I loved you less I should never give you an uneasy moment. – But hear me. – All my fretful doubts arise from this. – Women are not used to weigh and separate the motives of their affections: the cold dictates of prudence, gratitude, or filial duty, may sometimes be mistaken for the pleadings of the heart. – I would not boast – yet let me say, that I have neither age, person, nor character, to found dislike on; – my fortune such as few ladies could be charged with *indiscretion* in the match. – O Julia! when *Love* receives such countenance from *Prudence* nice minds will be suspicious of its birth. (*She exits in tears.*) In tears! Stay, Julia: stay but for a moment. – the door is fastened! – Julia! – my soul – but for one moment: I hear her sobbing! – 'Sdeath! what a brute am I to use her thus! Yet stay. – Ay – she is coming now: – how little resolution there is in women! – how a few soft words can turn them! – No, faith! – she is *not* coming either. – Why, Julia – my love – say but that you forgive me – come but to tell me that – now this is being *too* resentful: stay! she *is* coming to – I thought she would – no *steadiness* in anything! her going away must have been a mere trick then – she sha'n't see that I was hurt by it. – I'll affect indifference – (*Hums a tune: then listens.*) – No – Zounds! she's *not* coming! – nor don't intend it, I suppose. – This is not *steadiness* but *obstinacy*! Yet I deserve it. – What, after so long an absence to quarrel with her tenderness! – 'twas barbarous and unmanly! – I should be ashamed to see her now. – I'll wait till her just resentment is abated – and when I distress her so again, may I lose her for ever! and be linked instead to some antique virago, whose gnawing passions and long hoarded spleen shall make me curse my folly half the day and all the night. (*Exit.*)

Dabler from *The Witlings* by Fanny Burney

Fanny Burney was a witty and evocative diarist and a best-selling novelist in her day. She also wrote seven comedies, although they remained unpublished during her lifetime. Sheridan was a great admirer of her work and would have mounted a production of *The Witlings* 'sight unseen' had her father not suppressed it, fearing her wicked lampoons of well-known literary figures would scupper her own future literary chances. I believe the first performance of the play was the staged reading of my adaptation which I directed at the Tristan Bates Theatre, London.

The plot of *The Witlings* (those of little wit) is a variation on the 'portionless heroine' theme so popular in eighteenth-century drama. Cecilia Stanley, a wealthy, well-bred young woman, is engaged to Beaufort, adopted son of Lady Smatter who devotes her life to the 'Esprit Party', which is engaged in the study and criticism of authors such as Pope and Shakespeare, whom she indefatigably mangles and misquotes. When Cecilia learns her fortune has been lost, Lady Smatter forbids the marriage. Cecilia's efforts to avoid disgrace, Beaufort's efforts to locate and marry her, and Lady Smatter's efforts to keep them apart form the substance of the play, which of course resolves happily, but not before Burney has taken some satirical swipes at eighteenth-century literary life.

Dabler is an arrogant, pompous, oratorical, self-aggrandising, opinionated, posturing poet, 'an intolerable prating fool' who lodges in Lady Smatter's house and is much admired by the less than discerning 'literary ladies' of the Esprit Party. He will recite his dreadful verses at the drop of a hat, feeling himself to be one 'chosen by the world to be as poet'. Here, he is composing some verses in his room for the delectation of his foolish admirers, but is interrupted by the maid, Betty, who disrupts his train of thought, just as he has hit upon the bon mot to complete his 'masterpiece of drivel'. Exasperated that inspiration has eluded him, he stamps and curses before deciding to substitute a pretentious epigram – an epigram too fine for it to be passed off as the work of Pope.

Dabler is a splendid ham and the comedy derives from his ludicrous self-importance and belief in his own genius in the face of all evidence to the contrary.

———————————————

Dabler The pensive maid, with saddest sorrow sad, – no, hang it, that won't do! – saddest sad will never do. With, – with – with mildest, – ay that's it! – The pensive maid with mildest sorrow sad, – I should like, now, to hear a man mend that line! – I shall never get another equal to it. – Let's see, – sad, bad, lad, dad, – curse it, there's never a Rhyme will do! – Where's the art of Poetry? – O, here, – now we shall have it (*reads*); add, – hold, that will do at once, – with mildest sorrow sad, shed Crystal Tears, and Sigh to Sigh did add. Admirable! admirable by all that's good. Now let's try the first Stanza (*reads*):

> Ye gentle Nymphs, whose Hearts are prone to love,
> Ah, hear my Song, and ah! my Song approve;
> And ye, ye glorious, mighty Sons of Fame,
> Ye mighty Warriors –

How's this, two mightys? – hang it, that won't do! – let's see, – ye glorious Warriors, – no, there's glorious before, – O curse it, now I've got it all to do over again! just as I thought I had finished it! – ye fighting, – no, – ye towering, – no, – ye, – ye – ye – I have it, by Apollo! –

Enter **Betty**.

(*Starting up in a rage.*) Now curse me if this is not too much! What do you mean by interrupting me at my studies? How often have I given orders not to be disturbed? Tell me nothing! – get out of the Room directly! – and take care you never break in upon me again, – no, not if the House be on Fire! – Go, I say!

Exit **Betty**.

What a provoking intrusion! just as I had Worked myself into the true Spirit of Poetry! – I sha'n't recover my ideas this half Hour. 'Tis a most barbarous thing that a man's retirement cannot be sacred. (*Sits down to write.*) Ye fighting, – no, that was not it, – ye – ye – ye – O curse it (*stamping*), if I have not forgot all I was going to say! That unfeeling, impenetrable Fool has lost me more ideas than would have made a fresh man's reputation. I'd rather have given one hundred Guineas than have seen her. I protest, I was upon the point of making as good a Poem as any in the Language, – my numbers flowed, – my thoughts were ready, – my words glided, – but now, all is gone! – all gone and evaporated! (*Claps his hand on his forehead.*) Here's nothing left! nothing in the World! – What shall I do to compose myself? Suppose I read? – why where the Deuce are all the things gone? (*Looks over his papers.*) O, here, – I wonder how my Epigram will read to-day, – I think I'll shew it to Censor, – he has seen nothing like it of late; – I'll pass it off for some Dead Poet's, or he'll never do it justice; – let's see, suppose Pope? – no, it's too smart for Pope, – Pope never wrote any thing like it! – well then, suppose –

Enter **Mrs Voluble**.

O curse it, another interruption!

The Earl of Argyll from *The Family Legend* by Joanna Baillie

The Scottish playwright Joanna Baillie (1762–1851) was admired by Byron and was the protégée of Sir Walter Scott. *The Family Legend* was one of her most successful plays and received a celebrated production at Drury Lane in 1821.

Two rival clans, the Argylls and the Macleans, are united by a politically expedient marriage, when Helen, the daughter of the Earl of Argyll, becomes the wife of a Maclean, sacrificing her love for Sir Hubert de Grey, a friend of her brother, by doing so. The bond is cemented when a son is born. But hostilities are renewed when Benlora, the fiercest of the Macleans, is released from captivity and sees the peace as an affront. Benlora and other Maclean nobles devise a plot to murder Helen and reignite the conflict. Promising Maclean that they 'will not spill Helen's blood', they leave her on a rock to drown, but de Grey rescues her and she returns to her father's castle. Her brother and de Grey press for vengeance but the Earl of Argyll counsels caution, fearful for his grandson whom Helen has left behind on the Island of Mull. When the Macleans come to tell the Argylls that Helen has died of an illness, she enters and confounds them by being alive. A bloody battle ensues in which Maclean and Benlora are killed and their lieutenants captured.

This is the last speech in the play. De Grey has rescued Helen's child and they have been reunited. Benlora's lieutenants are in custody and the renegade Macleans have been vanquished. The Earl of Argyll addresses the assembled company outside the castle gates. He is an honourable nobleman in his middle years – the even-handed, fair-minded chieftain of his clan. This is a rallying, states-manlike call for peace and reconciliation in which Argyll promises retribution for the wrongdoers, and extends the hand of friendship to his fellow Scots, if they will take it. It is a great sadness to him that some should waste their energies on internecine fights when they could unite in strength and common cause against their natural enemies.

He paints a splendid and terrifying picture of kilted Scots battalions marching to war to the sound of the pipes in this speech, which is written in fairly strict iambic pentameter, giving it a noble, stately measure.

_____

Argyll

Lead to the grated keep your prisoners,
There to abide their doom. Upon the guilty
Our vengeance falls, and only on the guilty.
To all their clan beside, in which I know
Full many a gallant heart included is,
I still extend a hand of amity.
If they reject it, fair and open war
Between us be: and trust we still to find them
The noble, brave Macleans, the valiant foes,
That, ere the dark ambition of a villain,
For wicked ends, their gallant minds had warped,
We heretofore had found them.
                                    O that men
In blood so near, in country, and in valour,
Should spend in petty broils their manly strength,
That might, united for the public weal,
On foreign foes such noble service do!
O that the day were come when gazing southron,
Whilst these our mountain warriors, marshalled forth
To meet in foreign climes their country's foes,
Along their crowded cities slowly march,
To sound of warlike pipe, their plaided bands,
Shall say, with eager fingers pointing thus,
'Behold those men! – their sunned but thoughtful brows:
Their sinewy limbs; their broad and portly chests,
Lapped in their native vestments, rude but graceful! –
Those be our hardy brothers of the north; –
The bold and generous race, who have, beneath
The frozen circle and the burning line,
The rights and freedom of our native land
Undauntedly maintained.'
                                    That day will come,
When in the grave this hoary head of mine,
And many after heads, in death are laid;
And happier men, our sons, shall live to see it.

O may they prize it too with grateful hearts;
And, looking back on these our stormy days
Of other years, pity, admire, and pardon
The fierce, contentious, ill-directed valour
Of gallant fathers, born in darker times!

Don Gutierre Alfonso Solis from *The Surgeon of Honour* by Calderón de la Barca (translated by Gwynne Edwards)

Calderón is one of the great playwrights of the Golden Age of Spanish drama.

This play, written in 1635, is a disturbing baroque horror story about codes of honour carried to tragic extremes – a motif that figures in several of Calderón's plays. The chief protagonist is the Spanish nobleman Don Gutierre Alfonso Solis. Believing that his beloved, Donna Leonor, has been unfaithful, he abandons her and marries the beautiful young noblewoman Donna Mencía instead, not realising that the King's brother, Don Enrique, previously wooed her.

Don Enrique, injured in a fall from his horse, is by chance carried to the couple's house. He is distraught at finding Donna Mencía is married and leaves after an anguished reunion. Later, he visits her in secret and Don Gutierre's suspicions are aroused. Desperate to prove she is innocent, he disguises himself as Don Enrique to test her fidelity, but he misreads her reaction as guilt and determines she must die to preserve his honour. Racked with misery, he enlists the services of a bloodletter, Ludovico, whom he forces to bleed Donna Mencía to death.

In this speech Gutierre has run from the scene to tell the King of Donna Mencía's fate. Out of breath he tells a plausible story, devised to avert suspicion, presenting himself as a loving husband maddened by grief who has just discovered the bloodstained corpse of his wife, victim of a tragic accident. This is a man obsessed with the need to preserve his reputation, at any cost; a man driven by jealousy and adherence to anachronistic codes of honour which have subsumed him with terrible consequences. Nevertheless, Don Gutierre's anguish is real, and the love he expresses for Donna Mencía is true. His grief is almost operatic as his wife's bloodless corpse is revealed the court. The King, however, suspects Don Gutierre's implication in the murder and commands him to marry the abandoned Donna Leonor, despite his protests.

The speech is written in lines of eight syllables, with irregular rhythms and internal rhymes, a structure the translator has chosen in order to 'achieve some of the liveliness and musicality of Calderón's original'. Pay careful attention to the punctuation and give the verse space to breathe.

———————————

Gutierre

Your majesty, I come to tell
Of the most terrible misfortune,
A tragedy that cannot but
Demand for those who hear of it
Profoundest pity, greatest admiration.
Mencía, my dearest wife, in whom
The only rival to her beauty was
Her chastity – I say so publicly –
Whose precious life meant more to me
Than life itself, became last night
The victim of an unforseen
And cruel accident, as if
It were the whim of destiny,
By doing this to her, to rob
Her of divinity. She felt
Unwell, and so a doctor, known
Throughout Seville to be a man
Of reputation, thought that only if
He bled her could he bring about
A restoration of her health.
As it turned out, we had no servants in
The house to care for her, and thus,
When I went out, to keep an eye
On her. As soon as I awoke
Today I went to look at her –
How can I speak of how I found
Her there? – the bed soaked through with blood,
The sheets stained red, the wife I loved
Already dead, and all her blood
Quite drained from her because the bandages
Were not secure. Oh, how can words
Express such hopelessness, the pain
And anguish of such deep distress?
Come. Gaze upon Mencía there.
The fair sun bathed in blood, the whiteness of

The moon dark red, the brightness of
The stars and lovely music of
The spheres dead. Oh why must I
Be thus denied her perfect beauty? Why
Must loveliness like hers be ravaged now,
While I am saved and thus obliged
To mourn her loss eternally?

Rodrigo from *The Cid* by Pierre Corneille (translated by David Bryer)

First produced in Paris in 1636, *The Cid* is a tragicomedy by France's first great tragic dramatist. It was an immediate success and was translated and performed in London later the same year. The play tells the story of the lovers Rodrigo and Chimena who are separated by the enmity of their families, and is much influenced by Spanish stories of the heroic eleventh-century warrior known as El Cid. ('Cid' is from an Arab word *sayyidi*, meaning 'leader'.)

Rodrigo's father, the old soldier Don Diego, and Chimena's father, the much younger Don Gomez, are competitors for the coveted position of tutor to the King of Spain's son. When the job goes to the socially inferior Don Diego, Don Gomez reacts by refusing to agree to the couple's longed-for marriage and humiliating Don Diego with a slap across the face. Don Diego is too infirm to lift his sword to defend his honour and commands Rodrigo to avenge him.

Rodrigo is a promising young cadet from a long line of soldiers. 'Every trait marks him out as the perfect gentleman', and a good deal is expected of him in terms of honour, duty and manhood.

In this scene Don Diego has left Rodrigo with his sword and the command to 'avenge this deed!' Rodrigo is horrified. Caught between filial duty and love for Chimena, he doesn't know which way to turn. His hopes of marrying Chimena have been dashed and he is appalled by what his father has asked of him.

In this soliloquy he wrestles with his dilemma and the pros and cons of various courses of action, but how can there be a happy outcome? The speech is set out in formal verses, each of ten lines, which seem structured to take Rodrigo's argument forward. In the first verse, he spells out the torment of the choices in front of him. In the second, he argues that his love for Chimena should exercise stronger imperatives than the strict ties of blood. He is distraught at the thought of losing her. Perhaps, he thinks in verse three, it would be better to let Chimena's father kill him and put an end to it. He rejects this idea in verse four. If he is to lose Chimena, it is better not to lose his honour as well. Finally, he acknowledges his father's greater claim, reproaching himself for considering a less honourable course and steeling himself to do his duty whatever the cost.

Rodrigo
               I cannot move.
This blow bites so deep, it cuts me in two!
To avenge my father, I'll lose Chimena:
He spurs my honour, while she pulls me back;
               This puts me on the rack
For whatever choice I make will shame or
Shatter me – either way I'm sure to lose.
               Oh, you heavens above,
I've a father who's been grossly abused
And the culprit is the father of my love.

               This weapon's cruel:
Used, it kills my joy; not used, the jewel
Reputation's lost, failing to defend
The honour of my father, a son's duty.
               But what of love's beauty?
Chimena, in my heart, wields in the end
As strong a power and could well displace
               The rigid rule of blood.
Must I then use this to avenge our disgrace
And so surrender up all hope of love?

               I am trapped
And think surrender to death more apt
For, each way I turn, the noose grows tighter:
I owe to Chimena as strong a debt
               As to my father, yet
How he'll scorn me if I don't fight her
Father, and how she'll hate me if I do!
               This dilemma's enough
To make me let her father run me through!
That way at least I would not hurt my love.

               So to die?
A dishonourable death that would cry

Shame on my memory and bring disgrace
On a family to which I'd turned traitor!
                    Madness to placate her
Whose love I'm bound to lose in any case!
No! I must dispel such an idea
                    And lift myself above
Such folly. At least I'll keep my honour clear,
For either way there is no hope for love.

                    I was wrong
And reproach myself for taking so long
To see my father has the greater claim:
He gave me life and I will lay it down
                    For him, be killed or drown
After in my grief. I am much to blame
For this hesitation. But now it's over
                    For by the gods above
I'll punish this man who's wronged my father
Even though he's the father of my love.

Arnolphe from *The School for Wives* by Molière (translated by Richard Wilbur)

This lively satirical comedy was first performed at the Palais-Royal in 1662, with Molière himself playing the central character – wealthy, middle-aged roué, Monsieur Arnolphe.

Arnolphe, who has long resisted marriage, returns home after a short absence to announce his intention to marry Agnès, his obedient little ward whom he has raised from infancy to be ignorant of the wicked ways of the world. He has it all worked out. Marriage to such a sweet, dependent girl will be his guarantee against being cuckolded.

But when Horace, the handsome son of an old friend, comes to visit, he confides in Arnolphe that he has fallen in love with a beautiful young woman who is kept a virtual prisoner by her guardian, an 'aristocrat' called Monsieur de la Souche – not realising this is a name the arrogant Arnolphe has recently adopted. Arnolphe listens with alarm as Horace waxes lyrical about Agnès and tells him how he intends to steal her away.

After Horace has revealed their escape plan, Arnolphe is left alone to explode over what he has just heard. He is an egomaniacal control freak and absolutely beside himself to learn of the couple's secret meetings and future plans. He rehearses his arguments, confirming their self-righteous validity. This comic monster is subsumed by jealousy, furious at being laughed at, racked by the fear of being cuckolded and determined that his plans to marry Agnès will not be thwarted. The battle lines are drawn. Forewarned is forearmed, and his obsessive determination to prevail is only matched by his sense of grievance at being frustrated by a couple of 'wet behind the ears' youngsters.

This translation, like Molière's original, is in rhyming couplets, which can be a problem for actors. How to make them sound like 'real talk' is the challenge. Be led by the punctuation, the meaning and bombastic self-righteousness of the character, rather than the line endings, otherwise the dialogue will sound very sing-song and stilted.

Arnolphe

The evil star that's hounding me to death
Gives me no time in which to catch my breath!
Must I, again and again, be forced to see
My measures foiled through their complicity?
Shall I, at my ripe age, be duped, forsooth,
By a green girl and by a harebrained youth?
For twenty years I've sagely contemplated
The woeful lives of men unwisely mated,
And analysed with care the slips whereby
The best-planned marriages have gone awry;
Thus schooled by others' failures, I felt that I'd
Be able, when I chose to take a bride,
To ward off all mischance, and be protected
From griefs to which so many are subjected.
I took, to that end, all the shrewd and wise
Precautions which experience could devise;
Yet, as if fate had made the stern decision
That no man living should escape derision,
I find, for all my pondering of this
Great matter, all my keen analysis,
The twenty years and more which I have spent
In planning to escape that embarrassment
So many husbands suffer from today,
That I'm as badly victimized as they.
But no, damned fate, I challenge your decree!
The lovely prize is in my custody,
And though her heart's been filched by that young pest,
I guarantee that he'll not get the rest,
And that this evening's gallant rendezvous
Won't go as smoothly as they'd like it to.
There's one good thing about my present fix –
That I'm forewarned of all my rival's tricks,
And that this oaf who's aiming to undo me
Confesses all his bad intentions to me.

Tartuffe from *Tartuffe* by Molière (translated by Christopher Hampton)

Written in 1664, this is a comic satire on religious bigotry, vanity, hypocrisy and greed set in seventeenth-century Catholic France. Molière's genius lay in exposing the follies and hypocrisies of French society through satire, but the play proved so controversial that it was banned from the public stage until 1667.

Tartuffe, posing as a religious zealot, has wormed his way into the affections of the wealthy nobleman Orgon, who has installed him in his household in order to exercise control over his family and offer an example of piety.

Tartuffe is an unappetising young man – 'red ears', 'florid face', 'off the side of Notre Dame!' – with a keen eye for a victim. He is vain, devious, unctuous, manipulative, sly, self-righteous, eloquent, snobbish and completely amoral. His bogus religious fervour is laid on with a trowel and he has convinced the gullible Orgon he offers 'a gateway to heaven'. Orgon is completely taken in – although it is clear to everyone else that Tartuffe is a bigoted sanctimonious fraud, with an eye to fleecing Orgon of everything.

When Orgon determines to marry off his horrified daughter Mariane to Tartuffe, in spite of her love for Valère, the whole family is up in arms. Mariane's stepmother, Elmire, seeks out Tartuffe to beg him to refuse Mariane, but the pious villain responds by trying to seduce her.

In these linked speeches Tartuffe makes his play. He is at pains to convince Elmire that there is no contradiction between religious piety and his 'love' – blasphemously asserting that love of such 'perfect' beauty is on a par with love for the Almighty. Look at the overblown oily superlatives he employs to flatter and endear, and the religious terminology he uses – eternal, temporal, creations, glories, salvation, etc. – to camouflage his intentions. This is a confident, if loathsome, seduction attempt in which Tartuffe demonstrates his considerable wiles to wheedle his way into Elmire's bed. Empowered by vanity and greed, and puffed up by past success, he offers absolute secrecy and discretion – so important to protect the reputations of people like them. But of course he has fatally misjudged the virtuous Elmire who cleverly sets him up for discovery, exposing him as the treacherous impostor he is.

_____

Tartuffe
The love we feel for the eternal beauties
doesn't preclude a love for what is temporal,
and our senses can easily succumb
under the spell of God's perfect creations.
His glories are reflected in your sex,
but in your case it's more than that, He's revealed
His rarest wonders and lavished such beauties
on you, we're dazzled, we're carried away;
and I can't look at you, you perfect creature,
without admiring the Almighty in you,
struck to the heart with blazing love in front of
God's loveliest self-portrait. Oh, at first,
I was afraid this secret passion was
a cunning subterfuge of the Prince of Darkness;
and I even determined to avoid you,
thinking you might jeopardize my salvation.
But finally I realized, my sweet beauty:
in such a feeling there could be no guilt,
it could be reconciled with purity,
and that's when I surrendered myself to it.
I confess, it is very bold of me
to dare to offer you my love like this;
but I'm relying wholly on your kindness,
rather than on my own unworthiness.
My hopes, my well-being, my peace of mind
are in your hands, my suffering or my bliss
depend on you, and only you can make me
happy or unhappy, just as you choose.

[**Elmire**   Well, that's a very gallant declaration,
if, to be honest, somewhat unexpected.
It seems to me you ought to have reflected
a little and held back from such a step.
A man whose reputation as a saint . . .]

Tartuffe

Why should a saint be any the less human?
Confronted with your heavenly attractions,
a man just gives way, how can he reflect?
It may seem strange for me to say such things;
but after all, Madame, I'm not an angel,
and if my declaration is blameworthy,
the real culprit is your enchanting beauty.
Ever since I first saw its superhuman,
radiant glory, you have ruled my heart.
The indescribable tenderness of your
divine expression broke down my resistance,
overcame all my fasting, prayers and weeping
and concentrated all my hopes on you.
I'm only voicing what you must have guessed
when I so often looked at you and sighed.
If you could bring yourself to show some favour
to your unworthy servant's tribulations,
if you would deign to stoop down to my level
and out of kindness offer me relief,
delicious prodigy, I guarantee
my eternal, unparalleled devotion.
Your reputation would be safe with me,
you'd run no risk of notoriety.
These libertines the ladies so admire
at court are ostentatious and loud-mouthed,
always bragging of conquests, of whose favours
no detail is too intimate to reveal;
their indiscretions and abuse of trust
degrade the very object of their worship.
People like us know how to love discreetly,
and how to keep it permanently secret.
Our own concern for our good character
acts as a guarantee for those we love,
and once you've given way, you'll find we offer
love without scandal, pleasure without fear.

Nero from *Britannicus* by Jean Racine (translated by Robert David MacDonald)

Written in 1669, *Britannicus* is set during the last days of the Roman Empire in the court of Rome's tyrannical young emperor, Nero. It explores themes of political intrigue, corruption and the abuse of power, and is fuelled by the unhealthy relationship between Agrippina and her son Nero, who owes his throne to her murderous strategies to dispossess his stepbrother, Britannicus, the rightful heir. It charts how Agrippina loses her position in the court as Nero turns against her in his pursuit of absolute power.

Junia, a young noblewoman, has fallen in love with Britannicus. In order to prevent their marriage, Nero has had her abducted by his soldiers. He spies on her as they drag her into the palace – action that takes place offstage – but has not reckoned on the impact her dishevelled beauty will have on him.

In this scene he is telling Narcissus, Britannicus' treacherous tutor, about his first sight of her. He is a man besotted. Junia's resistance, modesty and vulnerability have sharpened his passion and he is determined to have her. He takes us through his emotional journey, from her helpless arrival at the palace to his sleepless thought processes, as he rehearses hollow expressions of remorse. Nero's instability, megalomania and depravity are well documented – he is used to getting what he wants, however unscrupulous he has to be to get it. Nothing he says can be taken at face value. Everything has a subtext of self-interest and manipulation.

Britannicus is written in rhyming couplets. Within the vagaries of the English language, the translator has largely stuck to Racine's original twelve-syllable meter. Pay close attention to the rhyme, punctuation and line endings. These are valuable guides to character, pacing and shifts in thought process. Consider, for instance, the dashes before '– but I was made weak' and '– I could not speak'. Or the ellipsis after 'but no . . .' What do these tell you about delivery, pace and Nero's state of mind?

Nero

Drawn along by curiosity,
Last night I watched them bring her here, I watched as she
Raised her sad eyes to heaven, eyes that shone with tears,
Radiant amid the tumult, the torches and the jeers,
Beautiful, unadorned, in the dishevelled dress
Of one who's dragged from sleep to painful wakefulness.
I don't know if it was the unaccustomed violence,
The sudden shouts, the shadows, then the frightening silence,
The brutal looks of her abductors, taken with
Her disarray, combined with all the rest to give
An added, helpless beauty to her – but I was made weak
By the sight, I tried to talk to her – I could not speak,
I could not stir. Struck dumb, astonished, I stood by,
Let her go to her chamber undisturbed, while I
Went to my own, and there, torn by self-doubt
And longing, tried in vain to blot her image out.
It would not leave me. I thought I spoke to her, but no . . .
I even loved those tears that I had caused to flow.
Sometimes, too late now, I would beg her to forgive me;
I wept, I even threatened, to force her to believe me.
Rehearsing all the sleepless night what I might say,
Enveloped in my love, I waited for the day.
Perhaps I was mistaken. Do I exaggerate?
Her beauty – was it just a trick of flattering light?
What do you think, Narcissus?

Figaro from *The Marriage of Figaro* by Beaumarchais (translated by John Wood)

Written in 1781, *The Marriage of Figaro* waited three years for its first performance at the Comédie-Française after Louis XVI banned it, declaring it should never be performed. Lampooning the French class system in its portrayal of a lecherous, incompetent aristocrat outwitted by a crafty manservant, it foreshadowed the French Revolution of 1789.

Its convoluted plot takes place in Count Almaviva's castle near Seville (the content too sensitive to set in France). Figaro, Count Almaviva's valet, and Suzanne, the Countess's feisty maid, are about to be married, but Figaro has learned that the Count plans to exercise his 'droit de seigneur' (the right of the feudal lord to sleep with the brides of his servants on the wedding night) – now he understands why his master gave them a lavish dowry and a bedroom adjoining his own! After a saucy exchange of kisses, Figaro is left alone to marvel at his beloved's charms and take stock of the interesting situation.

Figaro is a force to be reckoned with. He is irrepressible, impertinent, utterly charming, good-humoured, carefree and handsome – a larger-than-life character who knows he is more than a match for his masters in brains if not in breeding. Figaro lives for the pleasure of the moment, and relishes any opportunity for intrigue or advancement. He is already scheming how he can turn the tables on the Count, pocket his money and at the same time get back at Bazile, Suzanne's singing teacher, who has been acting as the Count's pimp during singing lessons.

(Beaumarchais left a helpful little note about the role: 'If [the actor] sees in it anything other than good sense seasoned with gaiety and sallies of wit – above all if he introduces any element of caricature – he will diminish the effect . . .')

All ends happily with Figaro's marriage to Suzanne and a contrite Count's reunion with his neglected Countess – a victory of ability over birthright!

Figaro Dear charming girl! For ever laughing, blooming, full of gaiety and wit, loving and wholly delightful! And yet prudent. (*Walks up and down rubbing his forehead.*) And so, Your Lordship, you would do me down, would you! I wondered why, having put me in charge of the household, he wanted to take me with him on his embassy and make me his courier. I have got the idea, Your Highness! It's a triple promotion! You – Minister Plenipotentiary, me – the breakneck postilion, Suzie – lady of the back stairs and pocket ambassadress! And then, off you go, courier! While I'm galloping in one direction you'll be progressing nicely in another – with my little wife! I shall be fighting my way through rain and mud for the greater glory of your family while you are condescending to cooperate in the increase of mine. A pretty sort of reciprocity! But it's going too far, My Lord! To be doing both your master's job and your valet's at the same time, representing the King – and myself – at a foreign court is overdoing it. It's too much by half! As for you, Bazile, you dirty old dog, I'll teach you to run with the hounds, I'll – no, we shall have to dissimulate if we are to use one against the other. Look to the day's work, Master Figaro! First bring forward the hour of your wedding to make sure of the ceremony taking place, head off Marceline who's so deucedly fond of you, pocket the money and the presents, thwart His Lordship's little game, give Master Bazile a good thrashing, and . . .

Enter **Marceline** *and* **Bartholo**.

Ha! Ha! Here comes the portly doctor; now the party will be complete! Hello! Good day to you, my dear doctor. Is it my marriage with Suzanne that brings you to the castle?

Gennaro from *Lucretia Borgia* by Victor Hugo (translated by Richard Hand)

Lucretia Borgia is a melodramatic prose tragedy based on the legend of the Borgias. It is set in sixteenth-century Italy and was first performed in Paris in 1833.

The infamous Borgias are a byword for butchery, sexual perversity and machiavellian politics. Born into a family where treachery, adultery, murder, incest and betrayal were the norm, Lucretia has emerged a depraved and pitiless woman. Her only saving grace is her love for her son, Gennaro, to whom she gave birth in secret and hid to protect him from her villainous relatives.

At the beginning of the play Lucretia has come to Venice in disguise to be reunited with Gennaro, now a twenty-year-old soldier blissfully unaware of his parentage. Gennaro's life is driven by his love for the mother he has never seen, and his desire to be worthy of her. When Lucretia declares her love for him, Gennaro feels a deep attraction for this beautiful woman and shares his feelings with her – unaware of her identity. When his friends learn of this 'romantic' encounter they name her as the notorious Lucretia Borgia, a woman who evokes fear and horror across Italy. Gennaro is repelled and Lucretia vows to take her revenge on his friends for betraying her and alienating Gennaro.

In this scene Gennaro and friends have been dispatched to Ferrara as part of a Venetian delegation. Lucretia is a powerful and dangerous force in the city. Gennaro has been tricked into wearing Lucretia's 'favour' and he has even taken lodgings opposite her balcony! Furious that he has been duped, Gennaro tears off the scarf and tramples on it in disgust, cursing her name and vowing to take revenge on her for all her evil deeds. He is drawn to her but repulsed by her – disgusted by the thought of her love, but haunted by an unnatural obsession with her since their meeting. He can't get her out of his head and is trying to rationalise his obsession to himself and to his friends. He is fuelled by emotions he can neither name nor articulate as he gives vent in this towering tirade.

Gennaro Oh, cursed be that Lucretia Borgia! You say that she loves me? Well! So much the better! Let that be her punishment! She fills me with horror! Yes, she fills me with horror! You know what I mean: it is impossible to be indifferent to a woman who loves you. You either love her or you hate her. And how could I love *that*? Besides, the more one is persecuted by the love of that sort of woman, the more one will hate her. I am obsessed with her; she surrounds and besieges me! What have I done to deserve the love of Lucretia Borgia? It's a disgrace and a disaster! Ever since the night you told me her name in that earth-shattering fashion, you wouldn't believe how much the thought of that wicked woman disgusts me. Formerly I had only seen her from afar, at a great distance, like a terrible phantom haunting the whole of Italy, like a spectre looming over everyone. Now that spectre haunts just me, it sits at my bedside, this hideous spectre loves me and wants to lie down in my bed! On my mother's life, it's appalling! Ah! Maffio! She murdered the Count of Gravina, she killed your brother! I would gladly take his place, but as I am still alive I will take revenge on her! There she is in her execrable palace! The palace of lust, palace of treason, palace of assassination, palace of adultery, palace of incest, palace of every crime imaginable, the palace of Lucretia Borgia! Oh! I may not be able to stamp the mark of infamy on that obscene woman's forehead, but I can at least stamp it on her palace!

He draws his dagger and removes the first letter of BORGIA *from the escutcheon beneath the balcony leaving the word* ORGIA.

Perdican from *Don't Play With Love* by Alfred de Musset (translated by Michael Sadler)

This is a comedy set in and around the Baron's castle in rural France, which Alfred de Musset wrote in 1834 when he was only twenty-four.

Perdican and his beautiful cousin Camille were raised together by Perdican's father, the Baron, and have been reunited at his castle. Both recently 'come of age', Perdican has just graduated from his studies (and a 'healthy' student existence) in Paris, while Camille has finished her more sedate education in a nunnery. The Baron, who has spent a fortune on their education, expects them to marry. When they meet Perdican is immediately attracted to Camille, but she gives him the brush-off. Nothing is more likely to fan Perdican's immature ardour, and what follows is a game of cat and mouse, with both playing hard to get with disastrous and unforeseeable consequences.

Perdican is a clever, passionate young man, caught in the confusing throes of his first amorous attachment. At the end of Act 2 Camille announces her intention to take the veil. Perdican holds no brief for cloistered and narrow education, and is full of angst that she is putting herself beyond his reach. Here, he has just intercepted a letter from her, addressed to her friend Sister Louise in the convent. His heart is pounding and his hands trembling as he wrestles with the temptation to open it. And the seal has already been broken. Irresistible! But the content of the letter is more than he bargains for. It seems to indicate that Camille has been deliberately toying with him. A plot has been devised with her pious friend to hurt and humiliate him. Incensed, he flies into angry 'denial' mode – his head arguing with his heart about his feelings. If he can't have Camille, he needs to convince himself that he never wanted her in the first place. What's more, he will convince her he is in love with somebody else. That will teach her and her man-hating friend not to cross him!

All ends in disaster when Perdican promises to marry

Rosette, a naive peasant girl, to make Camille jealous. The strategy works, but his hopes of happiness are destroyed by his guilt when the enamoured Rosette overhears the lovers exchanging vows, and commits suicide.

_____

Perdican (*alone*)   It is wrong to open a letter addressed to someone else. I know that. And I'm not going to open it. What can Camille be writing in a letter to Sister Louise? Could it be that I am in love? Has this strange girl some power over me? I hold this envelope in my hand. It's got three simple words written on it. And my hand shakes! How odd! During his scrap with Sister Pluche, Blazius must somehow have broken the seal. Unsealing would be a crime . . . but unfolding . . . Anyway . . . What difference does it make? (*He opens the letter and reads it.*)

'My dearest, I am leaving today. Everything has gone as I predicted it would. It is very sad. This young man will henceforth walk abroad with the pain of a dagger in his heart. I did everything in my power to make myself unattractive. God, I trust, will forgive me both for having refused and for having caused so much despair in consequence. Alas, my dearest, what else could I do? Pray for me. We shall be together at last tomorrow, and for always. I send you my most heartfelt greetings. Camille.'

It's not possible! Camille wrote this?! And she's speaking about me! Me? In despair at her refusal? Good God, if that were true everyone would be able to see it! What shame is there in loving? She did all she could to make herself unattractive, she says, and I am going about with a knife through my heart! What can be the point of making up this kind of story? Can it, could it be that the thought that struck me last night is indeed true? What are women? This poor little Camille, who may be truly pious, who may sincerely surrender herself to God, has nonetheless decided and decreed that she was going to drive me to despair! This was the plan hatched by these two bosom friends even before she left the convent to come back home. A plot! 'I'm going to see my cousin again. They're going to want me to marry him. I'm going to say no and the cousin is going to be heartbroken.' This is so exciting. A young girl sacrifices to God the happiness of a young man! No, Camille. You've got it wrong. I am not in love with you. I have no dagger in my heart. And I am going to prove it to you. When you leave, you are going to leave with the knowledge that I love someone else.

Osip from *The Government Inspector* by Nikolai Gogol (translated by Stephen Mulrine)

This satire about mistaken identity and corruption in small-town Russia was first performed in 1836 and is considered Gogol's masterpiece.

When the corrupt town council learns a government inspector, travelling incognito, is coming from St Petersburg to inspect the province, they are thrown into a state of panic. How will they identify him? Has someone reported them? Most important of all, how can they cover their dubious tracks? When they decide Khlestakov, a broke, jumped-up, none-too-bright government clerk staying at the local inn, is the likely candidate, they flatter him and wine and dine him like royalty. It is only after he 'cleans up' and leaves town, and the real inspector arrives, that they realise their mistake and anticipate a much deserved comeuppance.

Osip is Khlestakov's elderly manservant (though out of context and with a slight rethink, there is no reason why younger actors can't make use of this speech). He is of peasant stock, much brighter than his master and something of an old moraliser. Now he has reached the end of his tether as far as his employer's dissolute behaviour is concerned. Khlestakov has squandered his cash on gambling, drink and the 'good life', and left Osip starving back at the inn not knowing where his next meal is coming from.

The speech is addressed directly to the audience. A disenchanted Osip is lying disrespectfully on his master's bed, telling them about the parlous state of affairs his master has got them into. He sees no prospect of bills getting paid, or of ever going back home. He apes Khlestakov, as an upper-class young twit dishing out pompous orders to an underling. He conjures up a cosy apparition of simple peasant life. It would be better than this – at least he could eat. But Osip is clearly quite taken with the high life too – as long as there is money to be spent, respect to be enjoyed and cabs to ride in. Serving a rich master rubs off on a fellow, and there have been some good times too. You can be sure he will take full advantage of events when the mayor mistakes Khlestakov for the inspector and their fortunes are turned dramatically around.

————————————

Osip Dammit to hell, I'm famished! My stomach's rumbling so much it sounds like a regimental band. We'll never get home at this rate, so what d'you suggest we do, eh? That's more'n a month now, since we left Petersburg. His lordship's been chucking his money around on the road, and now he's stuck here with his tail between his legs, and he doesn't give a damn. He could've hired post-horses, he's plenty of cash, but oh no, not him, he has to make a show of himself every place we stop. (*Mimics him.*) 'Right, Osip, go and find me a room, nothing but the best, mind, and order up the finest dinner on the menu: I can't eat any old muck, I must have the best.' I mean, it'd be a different matter if he *was* somebody, but he's only a jumped-up clerk! Yes, and he gets matey with some fly-by-night, next thing they're at the cards, and he's gambled himself into this hole! God, I'm sick to death of it! I tell you, you're better off in the country: all right, there's no social life, but you've no worries, neither – you get hold of a nice peasant woman, you can spend the rest of your days stretched out on top of the stove, eating pies. Still, you can't argue – when you come right down to it, there's no place like Petersburg. As long as you've got money, you can live like a king – them theatre places, little dancing dogs, anything you've a fancy to. And they talk so refined the whole time, you could be up there with the nobility, near as dammit. You stroll through the Shchukin market, and the traders all shout 'Your Honour!' at you. You can take the ferry-boat, and you're sitting right next to a civil servant, no less. If you fancy a bit of company, you can pop into any shop, and some army type'll tell you all the camps he's been in, or what every single star in the sky means, so you can practically see 'em, plain as day. Then some old officer's wife'll drop in, or one of them young housemaids, and by God, she'll give you such a look – whew! (*Laughs and shakes his head.*) And the manners of 'em, dammit, they're so well-bred. You won't hear a single cuss word, and everybody calls you 'sir'. And when you get fed up hoofing it, you just hop in a cab and sit yourself down like a lord – if you don't feel like paying, well, there's a back door to every house, you can skip out through it and the devil himself couldn't catch you. Only snag is, one day you're stuffing your face, the next you're practically starving, like now, for instance. And it's all his fault. I mean, what can you do with him? His old man sends him money, enough to last him a while – huh, fat chance! Next minute he's out on the town again, riding around in a cab, and every day it's: 'Get me a theatre ticket!' till by the end of the week he's sending me to the flea-market to sell his new frock-coat. Another time he'll pawn the lot, right down to his last shirt, so's he's got nothing left but a shabby old jacket and overcoat. It's the truth, I swear to God! And nothing but the best English cloth – he'll lay out a hundred and fifty roubles on a tail-coat, then sell it at the market for twenty. And don't even mention his trousers – they'll go for practically nothing. And why's this, eh? It's because he won't give his mind to his work: yes, instead of sitting in his office, he's traipsing up and down Nevsky Prospect, or playing cards. My God, if the old master knew what was going on! I tell you, he wouldn't think twice: civil servant or no, he'd whip up your shirt tail and give you such a thrashing you wouldn't sit down for a week! You've got a decent job, so damn well do it! And the landlord's just said he won't give us nothing to eat till we pay for what we've had. And what if we can't pay, eh? (*Sighs.*) Dear God, what I wouldn't give for a bowl of cabbage soup! Honestly, I could eat a horse. There's somebody at the door – that'll be him now. (*Hurriedly removes himself from the bed.*)

Pastor Manders from *Ghosts* by Henrik Ibsen (translated by Michael Meyer)

Written in 1881, *Ghosts* is a domestic tragedy set on Mrs Alving's country estate on a fjord in western Norway. Many theatres rejected it in its day because of its subject matter, which deals with both venereal disease and incest. It received its first performance in Chicago in 1883.

Mrs Alving, the middle-aged widow of Captain Alving, a much respected chamberlain to the king, is making preparations for the opening of an orphanage in memory of her husband. To her delight, Oswald, their ailing artist son, has made a rare visit from Paris for the celebrations to honour his father.

In this scene Pastor Manders is visiting to discuss business matters relating to the orphanage, and has a disturbing conversation with Oswald about free love, open marriage and the bohemian life of a Parisian artist – views with which Mrs Alving expresses some sympathy. Pastor Manders is outraged, and when Oswald leaves, delivers this tirade, blaming Mrs Alving for her son's loose attitudes and censuring her for abandoning him as a child.

Manders is the middle-aged, pompous, self-righteous pastor of the local parish. He is a man far more interested in public image than in the care of the flock. Although he has been a close family friend and Mrs Alving's business manager for many years, he is hiding behind his position as her priest, wielding all the moral authority of church and office to reinforce the Victorian view that happiness comes from following duty rather than desire. The notion that there are ways to lead a fulfilling life outside the narrow values of the church is not possible. He reminds her of past sins – how, when young, she left her dissolute husband and he persuaded her to return by reminding her of the necessity of preserving her reputation and carrying out her wifely duties.

But Manders' pronouncements are rooted in denial. He chose to set aside rumours about Alving's reckless lifestyle in the interests of propriety, and underneath these pious pronouncements is a man who denied his own love for Mrs Alving twenty years earlier, repressing his feelings behind a wall of moral stricture on which his life has been built. He has proved a formidable adversary, but not without those qualities that made Mrs Alving love him when both were young.

Manders I feel deeply sorry for you, Mrs Alving. But now I will have to speak to you in earnest. I am not addressing you now as your business manager and adviser, nor as your and your late husband's old friend. I stand before you now as your priest, as I did at the moment when you had strayed so far.

[**Mrs Alving** And what has the priest to say to me?]

Manders First I wish to refresh your memory, Mrs Alving. The occasion is appropriate. Tomorrow will be the tenth anniversary of your husband's death. Tomorrow the memorial to him who is no longer with us is to be unveiled. Tomorrow I shall address the whole assembled flock. But today I wish to speak to you alone.

[**Mrs Alving** Very well, Pastor. Speak.]

Manders Have you forgotten that after barely a year of marriage you stood on the very brink of the abyss? That you abandoned your house and home – that you deserted your husband – yes, Mrs Alving, deserted, deserted – and refused to return to him, although he begged and entreated you to do so?

[**Mrs Alving** Have you forgotten how desperately unhappy I was during that first year?]

Manders Yes, that is the sign of the rebellious spirit, to demand happiness from this earthly life. What right have we to happiness? No, Mrs Alving, we must do our duty! And your duty was to remain with the man you had chosen, and to whom you were bound by a sacred bond.

[**Mrs Alving** You know quite well the kind of life Alving led at that time; the depravities he indulged in.]

Manders I am only too aware of the rumours that were circulating about him; and I least of anyone approve his conduct during his youthful years, if those rumours contained the truth. But a wife is not appointed to be her husband's judge. It was your duty humbly to bear that cross which a higher will had seen fit to assign to you. But instead you rebelliously fling down that cross, abandon the erring soul you should have supported, hazard your good name, and very nearly ruin the reputations of others.

[**Mrs Alving** Others? An other's, you mean?

Manders It was extremely inconsiderate of you to seek refuge with me.

Mrs Alving With our priest? With an old friend?

Manders Exactly.]

Well, you may thank God that I possessed the necessary firmness – that I was able to dissuade you from your frenzied intentions and that it was granted to me to lead you back on to the path of duty and home to your lawful husband.

Smirnov from *The Bear* by Anton Chekhov (translated by Michael Frayn)

The Bear is a delightful little one-act comedy. Chekhov described it as 'a piffling little Frenchified vaudeville' which he had written when he had nothing better to do, but history has judged it more favourably, and it offers the performer some wonderful comic opportunities.

Popova, 'a charming widow with an estate and dimples', is in deep mourning for her late husband, in spite of his cruelty and infidelities. She has vowed to be faithful to the grave and never again to leave the house. As she moons over her husband's photograph, she is rudely interrupted by the arrival of Smirnov, a handsome young landowner and former lieutenant of artillery, who demands payment of debts incurred by her husband for his horse's oats. The matter is urgent. The money is due tomorrow if he is to avoid bankruptcy. He is in a terrible state. He has neither washed nor combed his hair and is covered in dust and mud. Despite his entreaties, Popova declares she is in no mood to concern herself with money matters. Outraged by Popova's attitude, Smirnov refuses to leave the house until she pays him. 'Not until the day after tomorrow,' she tells him intransigently. Impasse! Popova plays 'the widow woman' to the hilt, accusing him of being coarse and badly brought up. He parries. She attacks. Exasperated and desperate, he launches into this tirade about his experiences of womankind, beginning by mimicking her criticisms of him. He is in a rage and clearly stung by her remarks. He has been unlucky in love, given his heart and soul to many women and been shabbily treated, so his defences are up. What monopoly do they have over the provinces of the heart? He becomes quite animated, so much so that he smashes a chair. But Smirnov doth protest too much, methinks. Popova's insults are already beginning to ignite his passion. He is quite taken with this feisty lady with her dimples and flashing eyes. When she later challenges him to a duel with her husband's pistols to settle the matter, he is completely smitten. Inside the growling bear of the title is a tender-hearted teddy, ripe for love.

Smirnov (*mimics her*)   'Coarse and not very clever.' And I don't know how to behave in female company! Madam, I have seen more women in my time than you've seen sparrows! Three duels I have fought over women! Twelve women I have thrown over – and been thrown over by nine more. Oh, yes! There was a time when I behaved like an idiot, when I was all sweet words and soft music, all scattered pearls and clicking heels . . . I loved, I suffered, I sighed to the moon, I felt weak at the knees, I melted, I went hot and cold . . . I loved passionately, I loved desperately, I loved all the ways there are to love, God help me, I chattered like a magpie about the emancipation of women, I spent half my substance on the tender passion, but now – no, thank you! You won't catch me like that now! I've had enough! Dark, mysterious eyes, scarlet lips, dimples, moonlight, whispers, panting breath – madam, I wouldn't give you a brass kopeck for the lot of it! Women? From the highest to the lowest – present company excepted – they're all hypocrites, fakers, gossipmongers, grudgebearers, and liars down to their fingertips; all vain and petty-minded and merciless; their logical powers are a disgrace; and as for what's in here . . . (*Strikes his forehead.*) . . . then forgive me if I'm frank – but a chaffinch could knock spots off any philosopher in a skirt! Look at one of the so-called gentle sex and what do you see? Fine muslins and ethereal essences, a goddess walking the earth, a million delights. But you look into her heart and what is she, then? A common or garden crocodile! (*Seizes the back of a chair, which splinters and breaks.*) But the most outrageous thing of all – this crocodile for some reason thinks its crowning achievement, its privilege and monopoly, is the tender passion! Because you can hang me up by my heels, damn it, if a woman knows how to love anything but a lapdog! All a woman can do in love is whimper and snivel! Where a man suffers and sacrifices, all a woman's love consists in is swirling her skirt around and leading him ever more firmly by the nose. You have the misfortune to be a woman, so you know what women are like. Tell me, in all honesty – have you ever in your life seen a woman who could be sincere and constant and true? You haven't! The only ones who are constant and true are old crones and freaks! You'll find a horned cat or a white woodcock before you'll find a constant woman!

117

Andrey from *Three Sisters* by Anton Chekhov (translated by Michael Frayn)

Three Sisters premiered at the Moscow Art Theatre in 1901. It is set in the Prozorovs' house in a country town about a thousand miles from Moscow.

The Prozorov sisters' recently deceased father brought them from Moscow more than a decade ago. Now they dream of escape from their dull provincial lives to a Moscow they have romanticised since childhood.

Their spineless brother, Andrey, has married a manipulative and ambitious local woman, Natasha, scuppering the family's hopes of social advancement. She schemes to eject the sisters from their home and is unfaithful to Andrey with one of his superiors. He had ambitions to be a university professor – but his soul-destroying marriage and a couple of young children have sapped his will and driven him to gambling. Now the best he can boast is being a member of the county council. He has mortgaged the house to the bank, without consulting his sisters, to fend off his creditors, and lost every shred of self-respect.

In Act 3 there is a fire in the locality. It is two in the morning. Everyone has rallied round to help, but Andrey just stays in his room, playing the violin. He is disturbed and angered by the disrespectful tone of the porter from the county office, requesting permission for the firemen to cross the garden to get to the river (he isn't addressed as 'Your Honour'). His sisters have made their antagonism towards him and Natasha clear and he is determined to have his say, in spite of their exhausted attempts to head off this self-obsessed, ill-timed outburst.

Andrey is worn thin by the drudgery of his life and racked by guilt at mortgaging the family home. He sets out his self-justifying preoccupations, point by point, like the government official he has become. But in spite of all attempts to present his life and intentions in a positive light, disillusion and disappointment have rooted in him like weeds and this empty defence of his existence makes him realise just how miserable it is.

Andrey I'll just say what I have to say and then I'll go. Forthwith . . . In the first place you've got something against Natasha, my wife – and this I've been aware of from the very day we got married. Natasha is a fine person – honest, straightforward, and upright – that's my opinion. I love and respect my wife – I respect her, you understand? – and I insist that others respect her, too. I say it again – she is an honest and upright person, and all your little marks of displeasure – forgive me, but you're simply behaving like spoilt children.

Pause.

Secondly, you seem to be angry that I'm not a professor, that I'm not a scientist. But I serve in local government, I am a member of the local Council, and this service I consider just as sacred, just as elevated, as any service I could render to science. I am a member of the local Council and proud of it, if you wish to know . . .

Pause.

Thirdly . . . I have some something else to say . . . I mortgaged the house without asking your consent . . . To this I plead guilty, and indeed I ask you to forgive me . . . I was driven to it by my debts . . . thirty-five thousand . . . I don't play cards now – I gave it up long since – but the main thing I can say in my own justification is that you're girls, and you get an annuity, whereas I had no . . . well, no income . . .

Pause.

[**Kulygin** (*in the doorway*) Masha's not in here? (*Alarmed.*) Where is she, then? That's odd . . . (*He goes.*)]

Andrey They're not listening. Natasha is an outstanding woman, someone of great integrity. (*Walks about in silence, then stops.*) When I got married I thought we were going to be happy . . . all going to be happy . . . But my God . . . (*Weeps.*) My dear sisters, my own dear sisters, don't believe me, don't trust me . . . (*He goes.*)

Acknowledgements

p. 10   extract from *Persians* by Aeschylus (translated by Kenneth McLeish and Frederic Raphael), Methuen Publishing Ltd. Translation copyright © 1991 by the Estate of Kenneth McLeish. Performance rights: Alan Brodie Representation Ltd, London (info@alanbrodie.com)

p. 101   extract from *The Barber of Seville & The Marriage of Figaro* by Beaumarchais (translated with an introduction by John Wood), Penguin Books, 1964. Translation copyright © 1964 by John Wood. Performance rights: please apply in the first instance to Penguin, London (adultpermissions@penguin.co.uk)

p. 86   extract from *The Surgeon of Honour* by Calderón de la Barca (translated by Gwynne Edwards), Methuen Publishing Ltd. Translation copyright © 1991 by Gwynne Edwards. Performance rights (amateur): Samuel French Ltd, London (theatre@samuel french-london.co.uk)

p. 117   extract from *The Bear* by Anton Chekhov (translated by Michael Frayn), Methuen Publishing Ltd. Translation copyright © 1988, 1991 by Michael Frayn. Performance rights: PFD, London (gsmart@pfd.co.uk)

p. 119   extract from *Three Sisters* by Anton Chekhov (translated by Michael Frayn), Methuen Publishing Ltd. Translation copyright © 1983, 1988, 1991 by Michael Frayn. Performance rights (professional): PFD, London (gsmart@pfd.co.uk). Performance rights (amateur): Samuel French Ltd (theatre@samuelfrench-london.co.uk)

p. 90   extract from *The Cid* by Pierre Corneille (translated by David Bryer), Methuen Publishing Ltd. Translation copyright © 1991 by David Bryer. Performance rights: Eric Glass Ltd, 25 Ladbroke Crescent, London W11 1PS

p. 106   extract from *Don't Play with Love* by Alfred de Musset (translated by Michael Sadler), Methuen Publishing Ltd. Translation

p. 13   extract from *Alcestis* by Euripides (translated by Gilbert Murray), George Allen & Unwin, 1915. Translation copyright © 1915 by Gilbert Murray

p. 23   extract from *Iph . . .* (*Iphigenia in Aulis*) by Euripides (translated by Colin Teevan), Oberon Books. Translation copyright © Colin Teevan. Performance rights: Oberon Books, London (oberon.books@btinternet.com).

p. 19   extract from *Medea* by Euripides (translated by Liz Lochhead), Nick Hern Books Ltd. Translation copyright © Liz Lochhead. Reprinted by permission of Nick Hern Books Ltd. Performance rights: Nick Hern Books Ltd, London (www.nickhernbooks.co.uk)

p. 15   extract from *Medea* by Euripides (translated by J. Michael Walton), Methuen Publishing Ltd. Translation copyright © 2000 by J. Michael Walton. Performance rights: please apply to J. Michael Walton, Drama Department, University of Hull, Hull HU6 7RX (j.m.walton@hull.ac.uk)

p. 110   extract from *The Government Inspector* by Nikolai Gogol (translated by Stephen Mulrine). Translation copyright © 1997 by Stephen Mulrine. Reprinted by permission of the publisher: www.nickhernbooks.co.uk. Performance rights (professional): Alan Brodie Representation Ltd, London (info@alanbrodie.com). Performance rights (amateur): Nick Hern Books, London Ltd (info@nickhernbooks.demon.co.uk)

p. 103   extract from *Lucretia Borgia* by Victor Hugo (translated by Richard Hand), Methuen Publishing Ltd. Translation copyright © 2004 by Richard Hand. Performance rights: Methuen Publishing Ltd, London (rights@methuen.co.uk)

p. 114   extract from *Ghosts* by Henrik Ibsen (translated by Michael Meyer), Methuen Publishing Ltd. Translation copyright © by the Estate of Michael Meyer. Performance rights: Casarotto Ramsay & Associates Ltd, London (agents@casarotto.uk.com)

p. 96   extract from *Tartuffe* by Molière (translated by Christopher

121

Hampton), Faber & Faber Ltd. Translation copyright © 1984, 1991 by Christopher Hampton. All rights whatsoever in this play are strictly reserved and application for Performance rights (professional): etc., must be made before rehearsals commence to Casarotto Ramsay & Associates Ltd, National House, 60–66 Wardour Street, London W1V 4ND (agents@casarotto.uk.com). No performance may be given unless a licence has been obtained. Performance rights (amateur): Samuel French Ltd, London (theatre@samuelfrench-london.co.uk)

p. 93   extract from *The School for Wives: A Comedy in Five Acts*, 1662 by Jean Baptiste Poquelin De Molière, translated into English verse by Richard Wilbur, copyright © 1978, 1977, 1971 by Richard Wilbur, copyright © 1978 by Harcourt, Inc., reprinted by permission of Harcourt, Inc.

p. 26   extract from *The Haunted House* by Plautus (translated by Kenneth McLeish and Michael Sargent), Methuen Publishing Ltd. Translation copyright © 2003 by the Estate of Kenneth McLeish and Michael Sargent. Performance rights: Alan Brodie Representation Ltd (info@alanbrodie.com)

p. 99   extract from *Britannicus* by Jean Racine (translated by Robert David MacDonald), Oberon Books. Translation copyright © by Robert David MacDonald. Performance rights (professional): Oberon Books, London (oberon.books@btinternet.com). Performance rights (amateur): Samuel French, London (theatre@samuelfrench-london.co.uk)

Disclaimer

Methuen Publishing Ltd gratefully acknowledges the permissions granted to reproduce the quoted extracts within this work. Every effort has been made to trace the current copyright holders of the extracts included in this work. The publishers apologise for any unintended omissions and would be pleased to receive any information that would enable them to amend any inaccuracies or omissions in future editions.